HULLAWRERR CHINA!

HULLAWRERR CHINA!
THE BEST OF FRANCIE & JOSIE

RIKKI FULTON
&
STAN MARS

BLACK & WHITE PUBLISHING

First published 2005
by Black & White Publishing Ltd
99 Giles Street, Edinburgh EH6 6BZ

ISBN 1 84502 071 5

Text copyright © Rikki Fulton & Stan Mars

British Library Cataloguing in Publication Data:
A catalogue record for this book is available
from the British Library.

Printed and bound by Nørhaven Paperback A/S

CONTENTS

Black & White Publishing would like to thank Muriel Mars for her introduction and for permission to use material from the early Francie & Josie scripts, including material from the early stage shows and from STV's The Adventures of Francie & Josie. The Publishers would also like to thank Mary Lee Milroy for supplying material from the Francie & Josie stage shows with Rikki Fulton and Jack Milroy. Thanks are also due to the literary estate of Rikki Fulton.

Proceeds from the royalties of this book will go to the Panopticon Theatre in Glasgow.

HULLAWRERR!

To make a new friend every day,
All you do is stop and say, HULLAWRERR!

You can chase the blues away,
If you will only learn to say HULLAWRERR!

You can make a sky of grey as bright as the dawn,
If you shake a hand and say, "Well, how is it gaun?"

The world will be a better place,
If everybody smiles and says HULLAWRERR!

McIlwham or Jones or Smith,
No matter simply greet them with HULLAWRERR!

The Frenchies greet each other "comment-allez-vous"
The English folk are famous for their "HOW-DO-YOU-DO"
But we prefer the pungency,
Of folks who speak the Glasgow way
HULLAWRERR, HULLAWRERR, HULLAW!

INTRODUCTION
BY MURIEL MARS

They say that Lana Turner was getting tore intae a large ice cream soda in a downtown Hollywood drugstore when a studio executive spotted her potentials and said, "Stick with me kid, I'm gonna make you a star." Before she could murmur, "Yeah, that'll be right", she was making a screentest.

Lana (sobbing into a hankie): Gee, I – I don't . . . don't know
        where to begin.
Cheesy Priest: Well my child, why don't you begin at the
        beginning?

Good advice that, but if you want to know how Francie & Josie got started you have to begin before the beginning . . .

Howard & Wyndham's *5 Past 8* summer show at the Alhambra Theatre, Glasgow was the biggest, the most lavish, most spectacular and glamorous production ever seen in Scotland. Beautiful girls with the longest legs, waviest feathers, glitteriest sequins and the No.1 top job for the comedian chosen to headline the bill.

In 1957 that honour went to Jimmy Logan and his co-star was to be the up-and-coming comedy actor from the Citizens Theatre, Stanley Baxter. *5 Past 8* was a revue-style show with a complete change of program every three weeks and that called for a lot of comedy material in a five month season.

Wanting all his stuff to be new, fresh and above all, funny, Jimmy approached a young Glasgow-born comedian called Stan Mars who, up to that time, had always written material for himself and his pal, Jack Milroy.

Out of his own pocket, Logan paid Stan a weekly salary and in return he got a steady flow of double acts, singles, front cloths and most important of all, a blockbuster sketch to open the second half of the show.

Each episode opened the same way. Behind a desk, a harassed police sergeant (played by Roy Kinnear in the days before he became a famous film actor and comedian) related what havoc and mayhem was being perpetrated on his patch by a gang called "The Hameless Ones", out there terrorising the citizens of Glasgow. Of course, the Hameless Ones turned out to be two wee boys – short trousers, scabbie knees and runny noses – played by Jimmy Logan as Shughie and Stanley Baxter as Sonny. Their criminal activities ranged from selling home-made lemonade fizzed up with Enos fruitsalts and picking daffodils from George Square to trying to sell dodgy souvenirs to American sailors. The sketches were a big success. The takings in the theatre bars suffered. The punters rushed back to their seats so as not to miss their favourite comics as two wee daft boys.

So, the following year, Logan went to do the *5 Past 8* show in Edinburgh and Baxter stepped into the top spot. Rikki Fulton took over as No. 2.

Stan Mars was asked to stay on as the writer for the new show and the big challenge was to come up with an even bigger, even better sketch to fill the second half.

SCENE: *A kitchen somewhere in Mount Florida*
CAST: *A Very Nervous Scriptwriter (V.N.S.)*
    His cousin

Cousin: Honestly Stan, what are you so nervous about?
Very Nervous Scriptwriter: Well, I'm due at Stanley Baxter's house in an hour. I'm going to pitch him my idea for the big new sketch and I don't know if he'll go for it.
Cousin: Well, tell it to me and see if I like it.
V.N.S: Okay – it's two Glasgow layabouts – the kind I used to see hanging about street corners when I was growing up in Oatlands. Workshy, always on the dole but interested in the really important things in life – burds, the dancin', football and getting a bet on.
Cousin: Kinda loveable rogues?
V.N.S: Exactly. I've called them Francis McKenzie and Joseph Tierney. Stanley would be Francie, happy-go-lucky and not too bright, and Rikki – with his long hackit face – he'd be Josie, the know-all.
Cousin: And just what do they do?
V.N.S: That's the point – they don't do anything much. They kinda hing aboot, philosophise and watch the world go by. I think they're probably a grown-up version of the two wee boys from "The Hameless Ones".

Cousin: It'll be a doddle. I'll wait here till you get back
           and you can tell me how you got on.

The very nervous scriptwriter returned a very happy
man. Stanley loved Francie & Josie and he immediately
came up with how they should look. He suggested the
Teddy Boys suits and wigs and winkle-picker shoes.

Here is part of the very first of the seven 'Francie & Josie'
scripts written by Stan Mars for the *5 Past 8* summer show
at the Alhambra in 1958.

FRANCIE & JOSIE
EPISODE ONE

Script by Stan Mars
Blacked out stage – Theme music is played which is
"Frankie & Johnnie". Lying stretched out on an
ottoman type couch is an American teenage girl.
She appears to be writing a letter. She is almost
immediately joined by her Mom.

Teenager: (writing) De-ear Francis and Jo-oseph, I was ve-ery pleas-ed to . . .

Mom: Hello dear.

Teenager: Hi Mom!

She sits up and makes room for Mom who seats
herself on ottoman.

Mom: Writing to one of your pen pals dear?

Teenager: Yes Mom . . . Gee, aren't I lucky to have pen pals all over the world? I have one in China . . . one in Italy . . . and one in France . . . but gee Mom, the ones I like best are the boys from Scotland, you know Francis and Joseph . . . boy they're for real!

Mom: But dear, aren't those the two boys who borrowed two hundred dollars from you?

Teenager: Aw Ma-awm . . . I explained that to you already. They only needed the money to give to a local Glasgow charity.

Mom: Oh . . . which one?

Teenager: I think it was . . . (scans letter) . . . yes, it was The Benevolent Fund for Aged and Decrepit . . . NYAFFS!

Mom: I see . . . they must be nice boys if they collect for charity.

Teenager: Oh they're swell Mom . . . and do you know they live in a Penthouse the same as we do.

Mom: Really?

Teenager: Ye-es . . . only they don't call it a Penthouse . . .

Mom: No?

Teenager: No-o . . . (scans letter) . . . they call it a SINGLE – END! And it's right in the most exclusive part of Glasgow . . . a place called COW – CADDENS! Sounds dre-eamy doesn't it Mom?

Mom: It certainly does.

Teenager: Money doesn't seem to matter to them.

Mom: What makes you think that?

Teenager: Well, they get all their clothes made in Italy.

Mom: They do?

Teenager: (flourishing letter) Yeah . . they just bought new outfits and they're Italian cut . . . Mmm, bet they're super . . . wish I could see them right this very minute!

Francie and Josie are standing near a lampost with Josie filing his nails while Francie is nervously fingering his outfit. Obviously he is a little undecided about how he looks in it.

Josie: 's up Francie?

Francie:	Don't know Josie . . . feel a wee bit stupid in the outfit . . . kinda hemmed in like.
Josie:	Listen Francie, 's the latest fashion . . . 's the latest Italian cut.
Francie:	Is it? Maybe that's what I feel like . . . a "poky hat".
Josie:	Pardon me if I'cream! Think of the glamour at the dancin' Francie. In this outfit you don't walk up to the dame and say, "Come on ah'll show you the flair – square!"
Francie:	No?
Josie:	No-oh . . . you glide up to her sort a nonchalawntie . . . and say, "Let's drift to Venice – menace!"
Francie:	Oh ah see-ee! Jings, jist wait till the jiggin' the night, I'll go right up to big Nola and ah'll say, "Heh Nola – here's yer Gondola!"

Blackout on Francie and Josie and the spots pick up Teenager and her Mom once more . . . Teenager continues as though conversation had never ceased.

Teenager:	And do you know Mom that they don't have the same civil liberties over there that we do?
Mom:	In what way, dear?
Teenager:	Well, it seems they have an Institution called the National Coal Board and they won't let this dear old lady change her coal merchant till next March . . . but Francis and Joseph are going to help her, they're going to do something about it!
Mom:	(rising) That's nice dear, I'm glad to hear it . . .

well goodnight!

Mom pats Teenage on shoulder then exits.

Teenager: (clasping letter to bosom) Oh but I didn't tell Mom what it is they're going to do . . . at ONE A.M. (mentally checks the difference in time) Gee, that's right now! (she gazes out into space and says fervently) . . . My heart is with you boys!!

Josie's face appears at an office window and he peers from side to side – he tries to open the window but can't so he starts to hammer on it, making a lot of noise. Francie now enters and walks nonchalantly over to the window, unlatches it and opens it wide – he then walks out of the office as unconcernedly as he came in, closing the door behind him. Josie stops hammering and peers after Francie in amazement – he next climbs into the office quickly and goes over to the door, opens it and in loud stage whisper . . .

Josie: Francie! Francie! Francie-Francie-FRA-ANCIE!

Francie: (pops head in window) Haw Josie? Aw, there you are Josie!

Josie: Sh! You'll waken the dead.

Francie: Why – is this a cemetery?

Josie: No it's the Coal Board! Quick, the tools!

Francie: Right Josie . . .

He throws in large tool bag which lands with a thud behind Josie who leaps into the air with fright. He turns and beckons to Francie who is clambering in –

Josie: You know just what you are, don't you?

8

Francie:	No, what am I?
Josie:	You are a silly bu'glar! Now then, keep quiet . . . SHH!
Francie:	SHH!
	Josie turns away and Francie taps him on shoulder and once again goes SHH! Josie just glares at him and carries on over to where he thinks the safe is and just as he bends down . . .
Francie:	Josie . . . Josie . . . !
Josie:	What?
Francie:	Where's the place?
Josie:	Will you shut up! I'm going to examine this safe . . . eh let me see now . . .
	He twiddles a knob on a radio and immediately a record of military march music blares out at full volume! The pair fall over themselves with fright trying to switch it off which they eventually manage to do.
Josie:	Phew! The trouble is it's too dark to see what we're doing in here . . . you pull the blinds down while I put on the lights.
Francie:	Okay Josie . . .
Josie:	Anyway Francie . . . you know why we're here . . .
Francie:	Oh aye . . . to help wee Mrs. McGreegor . . .
Josie:	That's right, these people here wull no' let her change her coalman till next March! . . . And she cannie stand the sight o' her coalman . . . cannie even stand the sight o' his horse!
Francie:	Aye she doesnie like Clydesdales.
Josie:	How?
Francie:	Came and lifted her television . . .

Josie:	Set no' workin'?
Francie:	No – her man!
Josie:	Well we're no' standin' for this carry on, we're no' gonnie let them corrugate wee Mrs. McGreegor! We're gonna open that safe there and register her wi' another coalman! Right . . . you get the tools out and I'll examine the safe.

Josie approaches safe in very professional manner, examines it, then turns to Francie who is at the tool bag.

Josie:	Uh-huh . . . uh-huh . . .
Francie:	's up Josie?
Josie:	It's the combination type . . .
Francie:	Is that bad?
Josie:	Well . . . it's no' the weather for combinations! Now keep quiet while I listen to the tumblers . . . (ear to safe) One . . . two . . . three . . .
Francie:	A-leary!

Francie pulls down a wall chart with pin-up picture of bathing beauty on it and printed on same, "COAL QUEEN" . . . He studies this avidly . . . Josie who has seemingly put on lights walks back to the safe.

Josie:	Francie . . . why don't you go and stick your heid out the windae – feet first?
Francie:	Right Jos . . . Awww, very funny.
Josie:	Get me the hammer and chisel.
Francie:	Here's the chisel Josie.
Josie:	Right . . .
Francie:	And I've got the hammer . . .
Josie:	(Placing chisel against safe) Okay, stand by . . .

	When I nod my head – you hit it!
Francie:	Eh . . . what . . . you nod your . . . and . . . and I . . . ?
Josie:	Fra-ancie . . . it's simple, when I nod my head – hit it! D'ye get it?
Francie:	Eh . . . aye . . .
Josie:	Stand by . . . RIGHT!
	Josie nods head & Francie hits him with the hammer.
Josie:	Ow ya! Francie, Francie, Fra-ancie . . . what are you trying to do?
Francie:	I'm sorry . . . eh you said . . . eh but . . .
Josie:	Never mind, never mind . . . just go and stand at the windae and watch for the police and I'll do this by myself . . . Now let me see . . . I could try the numbers consecutively OR one after the other . . .
	Francie peeks out window then goes to radio and turns it on. A tough, dramatic, gangster type voice fills the room.
Voice:	So there you are, eh! Come on stick 'em up . . . I said STICK 'EM UP!! Thought I didn't know you were here eh . . . Get 'em up higher . . . HIGHER! You'd better say your prayers ya dirty rat 'cause we're going for a little ride and only one of us is comin' back, see! Now take that!
	SHOTS FIRED
	Josie has re-acted to all the commands and "dies" when shots are fired. Francie has been laughing his head off at this, until another announcer takes over and says . . .

2nd. VOICE (BBC-ish): You have been listening to another

instalment of "DRAGNET" . . .

Josie: Quick . . . let's get cracking before he comes back . . .

They get back to the job in hand and get the dynamite and the plunger ready. Josie hands a wire to Francie.

Josie: Hold that . . . Feel anything?

Francie: No . . .

Josie: Must be the other one that has the two thousand volts in it!

He just turns in time to catch Francie as he faints forward.

Josie: Francie . . . I told you it was the other one that had the two thousand volts . . .

Francie: (Seeming to brighten) . . . Oh I see . . .

Josie has to catch him again as he faints!

Josie: Och Fra-ancie, snap out of it . . . right now we need something to deaden the sound . . . I know, somebody's jacket will do.

Francie: Oh, no' my new jacket Josie . . . it's hardly been on my back . . . hey, what about yours?

Josie: Look, does it matter whose jacket we use?

Francie: No . . .

Josie: Okay we'll use yours . . .

Francie: Josie . . . promise me it'll no' hurt the Lurex, eh Josie?

Josie: Francie, I promise you if there's anything left at a' – it'll be the Lurex! Okay, that's us ready . . . Stand by . . .

Josie is about to push the plunger down when he notices Francie with his fingers in his ears.

Josie:	's up? What have you got your fingers in your ears for?
Francie:	What?
Josie:	What have you got your fingers in your ears for?
Francie:	I can't hear you . . . I've got my fingers in my ears.
Josie:	Well take them out . . . TAKE THEM OUT!!
Francie:	Can't hear you . . . I'll need to take my fingers out o' my ears. (Takes fingers out.) What were you sayin?
Josie:	I said, "What have you got your fingers in your ears for?"
Francie:	But I haven't got my fingers in my ears!
Josie:	But you had your fingers in your ears.
Francie:	I know but I took them out!
Josie:	What for?
Francie:	I couldn't hear you.
Josie:	Can you hear me now?
Francie:	Only when you speak!
Josie:	Oh-h-h! Let's get on with it . . . Okay . . . get ready to blast . . . we're going to put one over on the Coal Board!
Josie:	RIGHT!
	LOUD BANG
	Safe door blows opens and out steps the Devil who says, 'Here, I want to complain about the coal I'm getting . . .'

It was the start of something big for Francie & Josie and the Alhambra audiences took the boys to their hearts. The theatre bars continued to empty as soon as the signature tune "Frankie & Johnnie" was played. HOUSE FULL notices were nightly occurrences and there was a suggestion that the management should provide a translation for visiting Sassenachs and American tourists. They always appeared to love it but probably didn't understand a single word.

Every change of program, the boys came up with a new adventure. Each one began with F&J's teenage pen pal (played by Ethel Scott, Rikki's wife) setting up the premise. In episode two, they visited a hospital, trying to sell their blood and almost operated on a patient. Episode three was set in Blackpool where they got involved in a black market cigarette scam. Next was a visit to Holyrood Palace, where they encountered Rizzio's ghost. Episode five found them involved with MI5 and Russian spies, and, after a visit to Paris, their final sketch was set in the USA, visiting their pen pal.

When the season came to an end, it was assumed that this winning combination would return the following year and repeat their success but new challenges were beckoning. Stanley was getting film offers and left to pursue his ambitions in London.

Several years on and, out of the blue, STV decided they wanted to get in on the act. Stan Mars was asked to adapt the existing scripts for television but a new Francie was needed, and who better than his old pal, Jack Milroy.

The Adventures of Francie & Josie on television was a hugh success. Jack and Rikki were made for each other. They became stars overnight, signed autographs, opened shops and mounted police had to be called out when they made personal appearances.

The first series in 1963 ran for six episodes. The following year they made thirteen and the same again in 1965 – a total of thirty-two episodes.

Francie & Josie consistently knocked *Coronation Street* off the top of the ratings so it seems strange that STV wiped all traces of their No.1 show from their archive, and today not one solitary inch of footage remains.

Up to this point, all the Francie & Josie material had been supplied by Stan Mars but now he had contracts to work in Australia then on to write for Universal Pictures, so a new writer was needed and Rikki Fulton took over.

The material presented here is a combination of the earlier, original work by Stan Mars and later writing and adaptations by Rikki Fulton, no doubt with some choice additions from Jack Milroy along the way. Francie & Josie were superstars of their day and I hope you'll agree with me that it's a real pleasure to relive in these pages some of the finest and funniest moments of their very long and distinguished careers.

THE SOCIAL CLIMBERS

Francie & Josie go to Charm School

Josie is reading Tatler magazine and Francie is reading a comic with a childish grin on his face. He bursts out laughing and Josie turns towards him with a pained expression.

Francie: Hey Josie!

Josie: Whit Francie?

Francie: Korky the Kat's really funny this week.

Josie: You don't say.

Francie: Aye! He falls into this wet tar, see . . . and a big steam road-roller runs right o'er the tap o' him! It flattens him oot like a pancake! An' – an' you know whit happens then?

Josie: Aye – they peel him aff the road, carry him hame and shove him under the door.

Francie: Aw, you've read it before.

Josie: Aye, years ago, when I was about seven. Of course, *I've* grown up since then.

Francie: Oh, I don't know so much. Only last week you wrote a fan letter to Bill and Ben the Flowerpot Men.

Josie: You never get *anything* right, do you? It wasnie to Bill and Ben that I wrote –

Francie: Naw?

Josie: Naw! It was to Andy Pandy and Teddy. Anyway, it's about time you put that comic away and turned your *mind*, if you'll pardon the expression, to better things. F'rinstance – the TATLER. I see here that the Countess o' Burntsugar and her charming daughter, the Hon. Fanny Cartwright, are enjoying a day at the races.

Francie: Is that her there Josie?

Josie: Naw, that's one o' the horses. *That's* the Countess.

Francie: Whit's that she's sittin' on Josie?

Josie: That . . . is a shootin' stick.

Francie: Shootin' stick?

Josie: Aye –

Francie: Jings, I hope it doesnie go aff while she's sittin' on it!

Josie: Of course, you realise why *we* are never invited to any o' these do's? (Francie shakes his head.) *We* are not socially acceptable. And do you know why we are not socially acceptable?

Francie: Er . . . Could it be because we've got – (whispering) – B.O.?

Josie: Naw, naw Fra-ancie! It's because we do not have any of the social graces. Y'know, like bein' able to tell Stork frae butter. And it's about time we did something about it.

Francie: Aye but whit Josie?

Josie: Well, I believe there's a fella opened up a sort-a Charm School, in Morningside. Think you an' me'll take a stagger up there an' have a few lessons.

Francie: But Josie, how'll we pay for them?

Josie:	Easy, we'll do whit the nobs do, we'll pay by cheque.
Francie:	*Cheque?*
Josie:	Aye, Provident Cheque! Come on . . .

An immaculately dressed man sits in his sumptuous office, talking on the telephone.

| Posh Man: | (Gushing) Why *cer*-tainly madam, I shall be only too-too delighted. Shall we say tomorrow at three? Splendid! |

Francie & Josie enter and overhear the posh man.

Posh Man:	A private lesson? But of course, how utterly *charming*. Au revoir! (He catches sight of Francie & Josie) Hrm! Er . . . good morning gentlemen. Isn't this a *charming* morning?
Josie:	Oh, definitely charming. And I suppose this is the *charming* Charm School?
Posh Man:	Yes-yes. What can I do for you?
Josie:	Well, we thought we'd like to polish up on our etticue. Y'know, sort a file aff one or two wee rough edges.
Posh Man:	You've come to the right place gentlemen. The object of this Charm School is to introduce you to a world of gracious living. You will become suave . . . debonair . . . cha-arming! You will learn the art of making polite conversation. "Ah! Good morning, *dear* Lady Millicent. (Francie & Josie turn to look for the fictitious Lady.) What sniffing weather we are having, what! I say, your melons should be ripe by now." See what

I mean?

Josie: Oh aye, aye – that patter should go down very well at the Palais.

Posh Man: Then, of course, you will also learn the meaning of deportment.

Francie: Deportment?

Posh Man: Yes.

Francie: Oh, *we* know a' about deportment – I had an Uncle that was deported. (Josie stamps on his foot.) Oooooh! Oh Josie, that was my saft corn.

Josie: It's no' as saft as yer heid. Er . . . carry on, Professor.

Posh Man: By deportment, I mean one's carriage . . . the way one perambulates . . . like so . . . Now sir, let me see how *you* would proceed down Princes Street, en route, shall we say, to the Usher Hall for a Symphony Concert.

Francie: Whit?

Posh Man: Come along – proceed.

Francie: Okay . . . (Does his gallas walk).

Posh Man: No, no sir! That would never do. You wouldn't *walk* like that to the Usher Hall.

Francie: Naw, I'd take the caur.

Posh Man: See . . . There's a rhythm to it . . . a grace . . . a flow . . . Now sir, let me see *you* walk as *I* walked.

Josie: Like that? Listen Mac, my name's Josie – no' Jessie.

Posh Man: Oh, my. You don't seem to realise that one doesn't just acquire charm, one has to work at it. There are all sorts of things to learn. For

	instance, a gentleman should keep his mind active, take up a hobby of some kind. Do you have a hobby?
Josie:	We-ell, I suppose you *could* say I'm somethin' of a bird fancier.
Posh Man:	Splendid! Foreign birds too?
Josie:	Oh definitely. As a matter-a fac', there's a wee foreign bird doon at the ice-cream shop the noo – just fresh o'er frae Italy . . . I often drap in there for a poky-hat.
Posh Man:	Ye-es, well, er . . . then apart from hobbies, one of the most important things a gentleman should attend to is his toilet.
Francie:	Eh?
Posh Man:	For example . . . how would *you* go about preparing your toilet?
Francie:	We-ell, er . . . er . . . I know how my mother goes about it. She just gets a big tin o' Harpic and a brush wi' a long handle – (Posh Man clasps hand to forehead.)
Josie:	Fra-ancie! You'll have to excuse him Professor, he got up on the wrang side o' the flair this mornin'.
Posh Man:	Quite, quite. But you will have to excuse me now. Er, *gentlemen*, I have a class to take. There is our Prospectus, you can look it over and, er, make up your minds whether you wish to take the course or not – Heaven forbid! Well, er, good-day. Tin of Harpic indeed!
Francie:	Cheerio! He should be on the stage. (Mimics

Posh Man's walk) There's a *rhythm* . . . a *grace* . . .
a *flow* . . . . . and a-*way* we *go* to the *Usher Hall*.
The Usher Brewery's mair like it.

Josie: Hey Francie, this Prospectus is very interestin'.

Francie: Is it Josie?

Josie: Aye. It says here, "How to conduct a courtship
with the opposite sex – young ladies supplied to
practise upon". I wonder if they turn up in their
practice dresses.

The door opens and two young ladies enter the room.

Primrose: I sa-ay, excuse me –

Francie: Whit? Oh! Hello, I didnie hear you comin' in.

Josie: Well, well, well, what *have* we here? Er . . . good
morning ladies, how *do* youse *do*?

Primrose: Good morning. We called about taking a course
in charm.

Francie: Oh well, the fella that handles that is through –

Josie: Er, whit my colleague means is that the
Principal is otherwise engaged at the moment.
However, *we* shall be only too delighted to go to
work on you . . . I mean er . . . to work *with* you.
Y'see, *I* am a Coach.

Francie: An' I'm his Assistant Coach – well, mair o' a
sort-a Charabanc . . . ha, ha, ha.

Primrose: Well, Mimsy and I – *I'm* Primrose – we . . . we
have a problem.

Josie: You could have fooled me . . .

Primrose: We've been seeing rather a lot of two young men
over the past year or so and well, they take us out

and all that kind of thing but – but so far they haven't . . . they haven't even tried to – to . . .

Francie & Josie: Ye-es?

Primrose: To, er, to kiss us good night. We feel there must be something wrong with us.

Josie: Sounds mair like there's something wrang wi' *them*.

Francie: Aye – it's *them* that should be takin' lessons.

Primrose: Anyway, we came along to the Charm School thinking we might learn something.

Josie: I should say that was *very* possible.

Primrose: Though mind you, Mimsy's already been to a finishing school.

Josie: (Eyeing Mimsy) Ye-es, and they would appear to have finished her very well.

Primrose: And I . . . well, at least I had a coming out dance. Here's a photograph of me in my coming out dress.

Francie: In the name! Here, you came out very well, didn't ye?

Josie: Well now, with regards to your problem, I fail to see how you two young birds . . . eh ladies . . . can be at fault but, if youse care to "park it" on the settee there, my colleague and I will demonstrate how an evening out should be conducted – with charm . . . and finessie.

Primrose: That will be *won*derful, won't it Mimsy? Yes, Mimsy would like that.

Josie: Ye-es – glad to see she's so full of enthusiasm. Anyway . . . ready Francie?

Francie:	Oh, definitely! – I'm with you Yogi!
Josie:	Right. First of all we call for you at yer hoose . . . we "chap" at the door . . . yer maw opens it . . . welcomes us in and says –
Francie:	"Mind yer heid on the lobby lamp."
Josie:	"Mind yer heid on the –" . . . Meanwhile, you two are upstairs finishin' yer toilet. Puttin' a wee drap Channel 9 behind yer lugs . . . gie'n yer hair a spray wi' the old Fairy Liquid – and *we* are holding a polite conversation wi' yer old lady . . . Francie!
Francie:	Ah! good morning Lady Millicent. *Spitting* weather we're havin', is it not? And tell me, how are your melons gettin' on?
Josie:	(With pained expression) Eh . . . yes, then we escort you to dinner where we go right through the whole menu . . . starting with Hor'ses Doovers. I summon the wine waiter "Eh garkon! Bring us four glasses of your very best V.P."
Francie:	Yes and *I* propose a toast – "May the skin aff yer back never cover a banjo".
Josie:	(Under his breath to Francie) I'll banjo you in a minute. After this, we go along to the dancin' . . . and this is where we finally come to grips . . . wi' the problem.
Francie:	(To Primrose) Here, would you like to come to grips an' a'?
Primrose:	I wouldn't say no.
Francie:	Well come on hen, the band's started . . .

Josie:	Francie! Fra-ancie! This isnie Seturday afternoon all-in-wrestlin'. Do not hold the lady so tight otherwise you will crush her corsage.
Francie:	Oh, I'm sorry miss, I didnie know you were wearin' corsets.
Josie:	Forgive my friend here, he just opens his mouth an' lets his . . . imagination run away wi' him. Well now, after a gay evenin's jiggin, we come outside the ballroom, pick up the "Rolls" – they're lovely an' fresh at that time o' night. Then we walk you ladies home – as it's a beautiful, moon-light night . . .
Francie:	An' besides, we havnie got the caur fare.
Josie:	We arrive at your abode and this is where my friend and I come to a gentleman's agreement. We toss a coin to see which couple are gonnie get the back close. *And*, having won the toss . . . (takes Mimsy by the hand) we take up our positions.
Primrose.	Oh, *they've* got the back close.
Francie:	Aye but don't worry . . . we'll go up the landin' and turn off the stairheid gas.
Josie:	Right . . . and now we come to the "coo de grass".
Francie:	Hey Josie, whit's a coo in the grass got to dae wi' it?
Josie:	And now Mimsy, this is where *you* lend *me* yer lips.
Mimsy:	Oh . . . *why*?
Josie:	Because mine are a' frayed at the edges. Look,

there's got to be a little co-operation here. This is the highlight of the evenin' . . . the good night kiss. You've got to *give*.

Mimsy: Oh . . . you mean like this! (She grabs Josie and gives him a long passionate kiss . . .)

Francie: Are ye gemme, Primrose?

Primrose: Ye-es, *I'm* certainly game.

Francie: Right, pucker up yer mouth. More . . . y'know, get it like the end o' an elephants trunk . . . That's it! Hold it – hold it! Fasten your safety belt, we're goin' into orbit . . . (He runs at her and they go into a clinch.)

The door opens and the students and the Posh Man enter.

Posh Man: Good heavens! What's going on here?

Student 1: I say, just a minute, that's – that's Mimsy!

Student 2: Ye-es . . . and *that's* Primrose!

Posh Man: You *know* these two young ladies?

Student 1: I should say so, they're our girlfriends! I say sir, you're an utter cad – that's my girlfriend you're kissing!

Josie: (Breaking off momentarily) Ach, drap deid! (Goes back to kissing Mimsy)

Student 2: And as for *you*, Primrose, I must say, I'm *most* surprised!

Primrose: (Breaks away long enough to jerk her thumb towards Josie and say) Ach, ye heard whit he said "DRAP DEID!" (Goes back to kissing Francie).

THE GOLDEN MILE

THE BLACKPOOL CIGARETTE SCAM

Francie & Josie are in Blackpool and are trying to make a few bob on the black market . . .

Josie: (Looking at the swivel headboard on the stall which shows the firm's name) . . . How's that eh? We're in business – *Francie & Josie*. Looks good eh?

Francie: Does that Josie . . . (turns placard at front of stall). Good, noo the shop's open! Think we'll do all right Josie?

Josie: All right! Francie son, this is the Golden Mile . . .

Francie: Why do they call it the Golden Mile Josie?

Josie: Well it's no' because Roger Bannister did his trainin' here anyway! Aye, aye, here's a customer, remember . . . leave the talkin' to me. *Man enters wearing slacks and open necked shirt.*

Josie: Cigarettes . . . get your cigarettes here . . . Five shillings for a hundred! A hundred for five shillings!

Man: Did you say . . . ?

Josie: That's right, sir, one hundred fags for five bob!

Francie: (tugging at Josie's jacket) Josie, Josie . . . ye goin' aff the heid . . . they cost us more than that wholesale!

Josie: Big Josie knows what he's doin' . . . yes sir, will

26

	you take a hundred?
Man:	Delighted . . . there you are, two half crowns.
Josie:	Thank you sir . . . (Gives them to Francie.) You're the cashier. Now sir, would you just haud oot yer haund and I'll drap the fags into it, we can't afford to wrap them at the price. Right now . . . ONE, TWO, THREE, FOUR . . . eh, been smokin' long?
Man:	Yes, about twenty years.
Josie:	Twenty! My, my, *twenty* . . . TWENTY-ONE, TWENTY-TWO, TWENTY-THREE, TWENTY-FOUR . . . just here on holiday?
Man:	That's right, got a nice boarding house along the front.
Josie:	Oh . . . what number?
Man:	Sixty-nine.
Josie:	Y'hear that Francie, *sixty-nine* . . . SEVENTY, SEVENTY-ONE . . . got the family with you?
Man:	Oh yes, even brought old granny.
Josie:	Did you? Well, well, brought old granny too, nice, eh Francie?
Francie:	Oh definitely, definitely. Good for the old girl, get her paddlin' her plates o' meat in the salt watter, get rid o' the old rheumatics like.
Josie:	How old is she?
Man:	Ninety-six.
Josie:	Ninety-six! Isn't that wonderful? *Ninety-six*, NINETY-SEVEN, NINETY-EIGHT, NINETY-NINE . . . ONE HUNDRED! There you are sir . . .
Man:	Thanks very much . . . (*He hurries off*)

Josie:	Ha, ha . . . Easy money, easy money . . . five bob just like that. Not bad, eh Francie?
	Francie has been examining the half crowns, eventually biting them.
Josie:	Fra-ancie, not bad eh?
Francie:	Naw – but the half crowns are!
Josie:	Whit?? Let me see . . . so they are! Can you beat that Francie . . . the dishonesty o' some people . . . it's folk like that who get the human race a bad name! It's a dirty, mean, low down, despisable trick, that's what it is!
Francie:	Y're dead right Josie, dead right . . . Whit'll we dae wi' them?
Josie:	We'll work them on the first mug that comes along!
	Glamorous girl enters wearing a Bikini and she's chasing after her beach ball. Francie catches it and shows it to Josie.
Francie:	Oh Josie look at this, it's a stoater isn't it?
Josie:	(Fyeing girl who has entered) Jings It's no' half.
Francie:	New Josie, here it's here . . . eh . . eh . . . whit are you looking at? (he has followed direction of Josie's gaze . . . he sees girl and his jaw drops open). Aw-aw-aw-aw J-J-Jo-ho-sie l-l-look, a WUMMIN'.
Josie:	New, is it? That's . . .
Francie:	Amazin', it's a wummin'!
Josie:	Naw – amazin' you could tell it was a wummin'
Francie:	Aw Josie, I could tell . . . I knew it was a wummin' right away . . .

Josie:	How?
Francie:	Well . . . eh . . . eh . . . she's got earrings on!
Josie:	Ah yes miss, right over here . . . Francie! (He takes ball from Francie and bounces it as the girl walks over to him.)
Girl:	Oh you have my beach ball, thank you ever so much.
Josie:	Not at all miss . . . Lucky for you I retrieved it before it skited intae the watter.
Francie:	Oh Josie, it wasnie goin' anywhere near the watter.
Josie:	(Looks at Francie as though he'll murder him – then smiles at girl and starts bouncing ball again) Ah how's about you and me for a gemme o' wee heidies?
Girl:	I beg your pardon?
Francie:	Aw go on miss, he's awfy good at wee heidies! So he is, so he is . . . If she'll no' gie ye a gemme Josie, ah wull.
Josie:	Fra-ancie son, I assure you, at this moment nothing could be further from my thoughts than a gemme o' wee heidies. Now then miss, where was we? Ah yes, you know, eh, something tells me that we are, eh, going to see a lot more of you this year . . . ha, ha.
Francie:	Jings Josie – you couldnae see much more o' her.
Josie:	Quiet Dracula! Now then miss, how's about a little momentum . . . to, eh, commiserate this meeting? Francie, give the lady a cigarette.
Francie:	Aye right Josie . . . here miss, have a cigarette

	. . . in fact have a few . . . and stick one behind your ear . . . and . . . and put some in your pockets! Eh . . . eh . . . (looks for pockets).
Josie:	Francie, the lady does not have any pockets. Now miss, can I give you a light?
Girl:	Eh . . . no thank you. You see, I don't smoke!
Francie & Josie:	Eh??
Girl:	But don't worry – I'll give them to my husband . . . Bye, bye.
	Girl exits carrying beach ball.
Josie:	Francie son, that's the second time today we have been taken for chumps . . . but somehow I think our luck is turning!
	Gump arrives wearing baggy shorts, white gym shoes, socks with suspenders, short sleeved shirt and cloth cap.
Francie:	Oh ho ho, ho ho, you never said a truer word Josie. Aw let me take him, Josie, eh, let me take him?
Josie:	Aw right Francie, he's all yours.
Francie:	Hello there, sir, eh, can I interest you in buying some cigarettes? We're sellin' them very cheap, five hundred for a shilling!
Josie:	Naw, naw Fra-ancie . . .

SECRET PLANS

FRANCIE & JOSIE MEET RUSSIAN SPIES AND MI5

It's the usual start to this sketch, with Francie & Josie's American pen pal and her mum. Teenager is lolling disconsolately on the divan as Mom enters . . .

Mom: Hello honey.

Teenager: (feebly) Hi Mom . . . (then sighs heavily, tragically).

Mom: What's the matter honey, aren't you going out tonight?

Teenager: Going out! What can you do in this dump on a Sunday night?

Mom: Well, there's the movies dear . . .

Teenager: Oh yeah . . . so there's the movies and there's the Open Air Dancin' . . . and the Downtown Jazz Club . . . and the Moonlight Casino on the river . . . and, and the Amusement Park – but after that, nothin'! This town's dead . . . now if only I could be with Francis and Joseph . . .

Mom: You mean, the two boys you write to in Scotland.

Teenager: That's right, Francis and Joseph. Y'know Mom, they tell me that on a Sunday night, Glasgow has to be seen to be believed! There they've got everything going full blast . . . they have a Mardi Gras in the Gorbals . . . and Water Polo in the Monkland Canal . . . and up in the Cow-caddens, they have a wonderful sport called, Middin'-diving! Gee Mom, it must be wonderful to be with Francis and Joseph, in Glasgow on a Sunday night!

In Glasgow, Francie has his hands in his pockets – Josie is filing his nails – there's a general air of apathy.

Francie: Heh Josie . . .

Josie: Whit?

Francie: How about goin' doon tae Waterloo Street and watchin' the buses leavin'?

Josie: Naw, we did that last Sunday.

Francie: Well, what about goin' up tae my Auntie Jessie's tae watch the television?

Josie: Francie, the last time we did that the interference was somethin' awful.

Francie: But Josie, I didnie notice any interference.

Josie: Naw . . . you werenie sitting beside Auntie Jessie!

Francie: I wish there was something we could do, I've weighed mysel' fifteen times already.

Josie: Here, tell you what we could do for a laugh. We could go into the Central Polis office and pretend we don't know who we are, y'know, tell them we're sufferin' from "magnesia".

Francie: Naw Josie, naw . . . I promised my mother I would never set fit inside a polis office, s'unlucky, dead unlucky. My Uncle Boab walked into one a month ago . . . he'll have seven years bad luck.

Josie: Ach, who said that?

Francie:	The judge!
Josie:	Wid this no' scunner ye though, ten o'clock on a Sunday night in Glasgow, dead as a doornail . . . I've seen more life in a flea circus . . . honest, I've had more fun at playin' kick the can in the cemetry!

Shots are fired nearby – they ignore them and Josie carries on speaking . . .

Josie:	I'm tellin' ye Francie, if Glasgow doesnie waken up folk'll start emigratin' tae East Kilbride . . .

Man has staggered on after the shots. He is holding his stomach and he clutches Josie's arm.

Man:	Help . . . help me . . . please help me!
Josie:	(Shrugging him off) Ach away and don't bother us . . . Imagine tryin' tae tap anybody on a Sunday! As I was sayin' Francie, whit this town needs . . .

Man has gone round behind them and now accosts Francie . . . hands over "secret document" to him.

Man:	Y'gotta help . . . Here, take this . . . go on, take it!
Josie:	Whit's that?
Francie:	Ach, it'll be one o' these tracts!
Man:	No-o . . . It's important . . . T-take it to Kelvin C-court . . . 88, K-kelvin C-court . . . Must go now . . . they – they're after me!
Francie:	I'm no' surprised!

Both of them watch as the man reels, staggers and lurches away.

Francie:	Powerful stuff that V.P.!
Josie:	Let's have a look at that . . . (takes document

	from Francie). Eh let's see here . . . (scanning document). Eh . . . hm?
Francie:	Whit is it Josie?
Josie:	It's a kind-a diaphram . . . s'drawn by a wummin'. See, there's her name there, MISS-ILE!
Francie:	Aye right enough Josie.
Josie:	Look at this, "Heavy Water" . . . whit's heavy water?
Francie:	I think that's what they get in Greenock when it's rainin'.
Josie:	(Reading with difficulty) It says here . . . Liquid Oxygen . . . . Nitrogen Fuel Tank . . . Concrete Launching Pad . . . Atomic Warhead! Heh, Francie, something tells me that this is not just a Do-It-Yourself-Kit!
Francie:	Naw Josie?
Josie:	Naw . . . these are the plans of an Atomic Rocket!
Francie:	Are they, Josie? Right, I'll go and get the polis . . .
Josie:	Not at all Francie, don't bring them into it . . . they're too busy pickin' up folk for throwin' away toffee papers. We will go out there ourselves and investigate, we will become heroes overnight . . .
Francie:	(Shaking his head vehemently) Naw, no me Josie . . .
Josie:	Francie, you'll be famous, you'll get your face in the press.
Francie:	I've had my face in the press – it's never been the same since!

Josie: (Grabs Francie and pulls him off) Ach, come on!

As they walk off, two men in raincoats and soft hats appear.

1st Man: Aren't you going to stop them sir?

2nd Man: No Jackson, I'm not – I have a better idea. We can't take those plans to Kelvin Court, they'd know right away that we are MI5. But they'll never suspect those two. They'll bait the trap for us, then we'll pounce!

1st Man: But sir, isn't that dangerous? They are liable to be killed.

2nd Man: I know, but what are two lives when the fate of millions hangs by a thread. Come on, we musn't lose sight of them.

Olga is sitting in a modern luxury flat, langorously drawing on a cigarette in a long holder, as she watches Max, who is pacing up and down forcefully. Max is dressed as a butler but is a tough, menacing type and wears an eyepatch.

Max: Half past ten . . . half past ten! They said they would have the plans here by nine o'clock at the very latest . . . What can have gone wrong? What's happened?

Olga: Who is the messenger Max?

Max: How do I know who the messenger is? Somebody, ANYBODY! All I know is that once he has delivered the plans we . . . (pulls finger across throat) . . . bump him off! Throw the body

35

into the Clyde . . . he knows too much! Then we . . .

(Doorbell rings)

Ah! This must be the messenger now . . . you know what to do? Keep him entertained till we get what we want then . . . (finger across throat again) right!

(Doorbell rings again and Max goes and stands behind door with his hand inside coat suggesting a hidden gun.)

Olga: Come in!

Door opens and first of all Francie peers round, then Josie's head comes round above his – they take in the scene and react to the femme fatale.

Josie: Eh?????

Francie: Oh!!!!!!

Josie: Hello there Jessie, ha, ha . . . Now I know why they call these luxury flats . . . will you just look at the fittin's! Ye wid'nie need an immersci to get intae hot watter here, ha, ha!

Josie is now on one side of her, Francie on the other – she glances imperiously from one to the other then asks Francie:

Olga: Who're you?

Francie: Fine – hoo's yersel'? Y'know, I think I've seen you somewhere before . . . in my dreams.

Max has closed door and comes up quietly to Francie and taps him on shoulder.

Max: And where do you think you've seen me?

Francie: In . . . in my nightmares!

Max:	WHAT??
Josie:	Heh jest watch it Mac, otherwise we will have to give you the message!
Max:	The message! You've brought it, good, give it to me! Give me the message!
Josie:	Well, I've been in Glasgow a long time but I have never seen anyone so anxious to receive the message.
Francie:	Whit would you like, two wi' the heid . . . or one wi' the bunnet?
Max:	Look, have you brought me the plans?
Josie:	Well, maybe we have or . . . maybe we haven't.
Max:	Ah, playing hard to get eh . . . you want more money eh? Ha, ha, right, we talk about it over a few drinks. Olga, entertain the boys!
	Max goes to cabinet to mix drinks.
Josie:	Olga eh, nice name.
Olga:	Mmm . . . a penny for your thoughts?
Josie:	As a matter of fact, I was just wonderin' if you were outside that dress trying to get in or inside trying to get out? Ha, ha, ha. . . .
Olga:	(To Francie) But what about you, handsome? I don't have to ask you what you're thinking, I can read *your* thoughts.
Francie:	Aw, naw ye cannie.
Olga:	Oh yes I can.
Francie:	Ach naw ye cannie.
Olga:	Oh yes I can, I can read your thoughts.
Francie:	Can you?
Olga:	Ye-es . . .

Francie:	Well, why have you no' slapped my face?
Olga:	I've got an idea, let's have a little music . . .
	Olga goes to radio and switches on – comes back again to the boys.
Olga:	Now then, wouldn't you boys like to dance?
Josie:	Certainly!
Francie:	Sure!
	Francie and Josie take each other as partners and start dancing. With Josie leading they do a foxtrot and patter while they do so.
Josie:	Eh come here often?
Francie:	Naw, jist every night.
Josie:	Anybody ever tell you ye dance like Vera Ellen?
Francie:	Naw . . .
Josie:	I'm no' surprised! Smashin' flair, in't it?
Francie:	Aye – wish ye'd get aff my feet and try it!
Josie:	You know somethin', you're one in a million . . .
Francie:	. . . So's yer chances!
Josie:	Anybody seein' ye hame?
Francie:	Seein' mysel' hame.
Josie:	Don't fancy yer joab! No' got a lumber?
Francie:	Naw . . .
Josie:	Where do ye stay?
Francie:	Coatbridge.
Josie:	Sno' a lumber you want . . . it's a pen pal!
	Max, who has carried drinks to the table, puts them down then taps Francie on the shoulder and says, "Excuse me". Francie says, "Certainly" and starts to dance with him. Max breaks away.
Max:	Bah, enough of this, let's all drink to the success

of our mission.

Josie: All right and (nudging Francie knowingly) we'll drink to the success of *our* plans.
Francie and Josie have two large glasses.

Josie: Eh whit's this?

Max: Oh it's something special I made up for you boys – it's called Volcano.

Francie: Whit's in it?

Max: Ach, just Vodka.

Francie: Oh that's all right, as long as it's nothing alcoholic.

All: To success!
They all drink and Francie and Josie are soon the worse for wear.

Max: Now to business, hand over the plans.
Both Francie & Josie act a little cocky because of the drink.

Josie: D'ye hear that Francie, he wants the plans, ha, ha, ha.

Francie: Aye . . . ha, ha, ha, tell him Josie.

Josie: Shall I?

Francie: Sure Josie, tell him.

Josie: Right . . .

Max: Look, I'm waiting, hand over the plans.

Josie: Naw!

Max: What did you say?

Josie: I said, K-N-O . . . NO! And furthermore, you foreigners come over here and think we're as daft as we're stupid lookin' . . . but we are no', are we Francie?

Francie:	Naw – we could'nie be!
Josie:	We know what your little game is and we are going to put a stop to it.
Max:	How?
Josie:	By lifting this telephone here, dialling 999 for the polis.
Max:	Don't touch that phone!
Josie:	Why?
Max:	'Cause I don't want you to!
Josie:	You'll have to give me better arguement than that.
Max:	(Producing gun) How about this?
Josie:	(Dropping phone) That's a better argument!
Max:	All right, both of you down on your knees, down! You know too much and you will have to die. You would try to make a fool out of Max, eh? . . . I'm too tough for that . . . (indicating eyepatch) What do you think this is?
Francie:	A sty?
Max:	No I lost it in a foxhole in Leningrad.
Francie:	That's funny, my uncle Willie lost an eye too.
Max:	In a foxhole in Leningrad?
Francie:	Naw – a keyhole in Garngad!
Max:	Before I kill you, have you anything to say?
Josie:	Aye, jist one word . . .
Max:	What?
Josie:	HELP!
Francie:	Josie, before we go . . . I hope we meet again upstairs.
Josie:	Francie, whit makes ye think we'll go up the way?

Francie:	Oh I never thought Josie, we might go doon below to . . .
Josie:	Never mind Francie, there's one consolation about that . . .
Francie:	What?
Josie:	It couldnie be any worse than Glasgow on a Sunday!
Max:	Right, I will count three and you will die. One, two . . .

Door flies open and the two MI5 types come through and start shooting it out with Max. The three of them shoot each other dead – but Francie and Josie who had covered their eyes don't see this happen but only hear the shots and they think they have been shot. They finally cling to each other desperately and whisper hoarsely.

Josie:	Where'd they get you old pal?
Francie:	I . . . I . . . don't know . . . but, but I only hope he has'nie spoiled my jacket!
Josie:	Francie . . . I can hear music . . . I can hear a heavenly choir.
Francie:	Can you Josie?
Josie:	Aye . . . and it's beautiful.
Francie:	What are they singin' Josie?
Josie:	(Sings) "You are my special angel!"
Olga:	Get up on your feet, neither of you has been hurt!

Both exclaim with surprise then get up and spot the other bodies.

Josie:	What happened?

Olga:	The MI5 killed poor Max. Now listen, you're going to be good boys, aren't you and give Olga the plans?
Josie:	Not on yer Nellie.
Francie:	Oh no, I've got them here and here they stay! (Pulls document from inside pocket and shows them).
Olga:	Now look boys, I can be very charming and romantic when I like . . . especially when the lights are out!
	Olga switches off the standard lamp and the room is pitch dark.
Francie:	Oh . . oh . . . the plans . . . Josie, the plans!
Josie:	Put the lights on somebody . . . Lights!
	Lights finally come up and Olga is discovered at the open door flourishing the PLANS.
Olga:	HA – HA . . . Look what I've got!
Both:	*HA – HA . . . LOOK WHAT WE'VE GOT!!*
	Francie and Josie are holding up a pair of pants and a bra!

CHINA-SHIP

Josie is sitting at a cafe table with a cup of tea, reading the newspaper. He turns to the Sports section on the back page.

Josie: Mmm . . . "Angry spectators invade pitch and tear down goalposts! Fifty arrests made!" They want to ban these friendly "Friendly" games!

Francie: (Entering) Hello Josie!

Josie: Hello Francie.

Francie: Where's Luigi?

Josie: Through the back. Er . . . I didnie expect ye back frae Prestwick so soon. Did your Auntie Jessie get off on the plane a' right?

Francie: Oh aye, fine.

Josie: Was she nervous?

Francie: We-ell, she was a wee bit nervous, y'know. So I took her into the bar and after her third nip o' whisky she suddenly stood up and said "Start the countdown, I'm ready to blast off!".

Josie: Aye . . . I remember her tellin' me that the reason she didnie like flyin' was because they might travel faster than sound and she likes to have a good blether!

Francie: Aye . . . 's just like her.

Josie: How long do you think she'll be in Canada?

Francie: Difficult to say Josie. Her daughter's had twins

	and she's gone over to help out. Might be six months – maybe longer.
Josie:	That's a long time for you to be lookin' after yoursel' in that room and kitchen.
Francie:	That's what my sister Margaret said when she invited me to go an' stay wi' her out at East Kilbride.
Josie:	(Alarmed) Eh? You're no' goin' away oot to East Kilbride? You might as well *emigrate*!
Francie:	We-ell, she was that nice about it, I didnie like to refuse. Besides, I can always come an' see you noo and again. 'Bout once a month – by "Well's Fargo".
Josie:	Once a *month*?
Francie:	I'm sorry aboot this Josie.
Josie:	*Sorry*?
Francie:	I'll write often, Josie.
Josie:	Whit's to become of wur "china-ship"? And whit aboot oor business transactions? Our sidelines? I've already ordered the novelty monkeys.
Francie:	Ye have?
Josie:	*Ten dozen o' them*! "Just flick your wrist and watch them twist" . . . I'll never flog that lot by mysel'. And whit aboot our football colours – the rosettes? "Wear the colour and support 'ra team!". We've built up a good connection there.
Francie:	So we have – even the mounted polis buy frae us. Look Josie, it's no' that I fancy goin' away oot there. I mean, where my sister lives there's nae closes.

Josie: (Incredulously) Nae *closes*?

Francie: Naw – if you take a lassie hame you've got to say good night oot at the garden gate . . . *very dodgy*! Nae cover . . .

Josie: Have you er . . . taken into account the fact that you will have to break in a new Labour Exchange?

Francie: Aw *naw*, Josie?

Josie: Aw but *aye*, Francie. All the privileges which you enjoy through bein' a shop steward at your present Exchange will go for nothing. Out there you will just be a – a number . . . ! Another face in the queque . . . ! A "stateless person" . . . !

Francie: Josie, you make it sound terrible.

Josie: That's the way it'll be, Francie.

Francie: But I don't like the thought o' stayin' in that room an' kitchen a' by mysel'. It's auld property an' when you're lyin' in bed at night and the wind's whistlin' doon the chimney and up through the cracks – well, there's a lot o' queer noises. When my Auntie Jessie was there, she would get up wi' the poker an' go and have a look – just to put my mind at rest.

Josie: Aye . . . looks as though the poker'll have to get up by itsel' noo! Unless . . .

Francie: Unless whit Josie?

Josie: Well, thinkin' back over our conversation, it strikes me that wi' all our business ventures – Francie & Josie Enterprises etc . . . and, er, our mutual respect for each others good taste an' ability in social matters . . .

Francie: Ye mean, like bein' able to eye up a couple of birds just like that! Then . . . *move right in*?

Josie: (Frowning) Ye-es . . . I suppose that comes into it as well. Anyway, it strikes me that our lives is "inexonerably" entwined the 'gither . . . if you know whit I mean.

Francie: Sure – we're stuck wi' each other.

Josie: (Eyeing Francie coldly) Let's just say that *I'm* stuck wi' *you*.

Francie: Suits me, Josie.

Josie: There seems to be only one solution . . .

Francie: You mean that *you'll* come an' –

Josie: . . . *only* 'til Auntie Jessie gets back.

Francie: Josie, that's smashin'! Oh but er . . . how do you think your mother'll take it?

Josie: Well, she'll probably have a wee greet to hersel' –

Francie: Aye . . .

Josie: *On the other hand*, my faither will probably hang out the flags and cheer! Y'know Francie, it's a funny thing about my faither but he's never really got used to the idea o' givin' me my breakfast in bed before he goes out to his work in the mornin'. I wonder why . . . ?

THE WALLET

FRANCIE & JOSIE FACE A DIFFICULT MORAL DILEMMA

Francie is in the kitchen, looking worried. He's pacing up and down and desperately searching his pockets for cigarettes. He finds a bent ciggy and straightens it out. He finds a match but it won't work and then he burns his fingers. He's having a bad day, then Josie arrives.

Josie: Ah ... ! Greetings, dear china – I see thou has at last got out of thy kip!

Francie: Josie, where were you? I went through tae the room an' the bed was made up an' –

Josie: Ye-es ... you were snorin' your heid off so I just went out and had a wee breath o' fresh. Y'know Francie, I wiz just thinkin' there, as I donnered doon the road, how marvellous it is to be in Glasgow on a mornin' like this.

Francie: Aye sure Josie but look I –

Josie: It's exhileratin' ! Upliftin'! A' that colour and spectacle. The rain glistenin' on the trolley wires ... The enchantin' aroma that wafts out as ye pass the tannery ... And then further doon the road ye see whit looks like a big Dalmation dug directin' the traffic but on closer inspection it turns out to be a polis, his white coat a' covered wi' splashes aff the buses! There are eight million stories in the "Glaikit City" – *this* has

	been one of them. Good, eh Francie?
Francie:	I–I wasnie really listenin' Josie . . .
Josie:	'Sup wi' your face this mornin'? You were full o' beans when you left me last night to take that bird hame. Whit happened – she no' let ye staun' up the close?
Francie:	Of course she did. As a matter of fact her faither came creepin' doon the stairs and got the hold o' me by the scruff o' the neck an' said "I'll teach you to make love to *my* daughter" . . . An' *she* turns roon an' says "I wish ye wid faither, he's no' makin' much o' a job o' it !" Bloomin' cheek!
Josie:	Ye-es . . . maybe *I'd* better see her hame next time. However, there's nae need to let a wee thing like that upset ye – it's whit's known as an occupational hazard among us . . . "bird fanciers".
Francie:	That's no' whit's upset me – it's somethin' else. It's . . .
Josie:	Go on . . .
Francie:	Well, after I left the lassie last night, I ran a' the way along Argyle Street . . .
Josie:	RAN?
Francie:	Aye, her faither was chasin' me.
Josie:	Case explained.
Francie:	Anyway, he gave up and I was just cuttin' through the Central Station when this fella and his lassie banged right intae me – whit a stoater! – the lassie I mean. I watched her a' the way to the ticket barrier . . .

Josie:	Ye can gie me her vital statistics efter – get on wi' the story.
Fancie:	Well, I happened to look doon and there was this wallet lyin' – the fella must-a dropped it ...
Josie:	A wallet?
Francie:	Aye – so I picked it up an' ran after them but the train was pullin' oot an' they were on their way to London.
Josie:	Mm ... Tell me Francie, was there er ... anythin' o' "interest" in this wallet?
Francie:	Oh aye! Had a drivin' licence wi' his name an' address on it ...
Josie:	Drivin' licence ...
Francie:	A few photy's ...
Josie:	Photy's ...
Francie:	Some thrupenny stamps ...
Josie:	Aye, thrupenny stamps ...
Francie:	An' a hundred an' thirty five quid in fivers.
Josie:	An' a hundred an' thirty – (lips trembling, he just manages to croak) quid?
Francie:	In fivers.
Josie:	Whit did ye do?
Francie:	I thought, best thing to do is take it along to the police station an' –
Josie:	Fra-ancie, you did *not* take it to the police station?
Francie:	That's right – I *didnie*.
Josie:	Phew ... ! Don't ever do that to me again!
Francie:	I got a better idea Josie. I knew the fella wid be worried losin' a' that money so I sent him a

	telegram – he'll get it first thing this mornin'. Did I do right, Josie?
Josie:	That all depends . . . on whit you put in the telegram. I mean, did you *tip your hand*?
Francie:	Oh naw . . . I was very circumspect.
Josie:	Eh?
Francie:	Circumspect.
Josie:	Where'd you learn that?
Francie:	Heard you sayin' it Josie.
Josie:	Oh! – in that case it must be right. Whit did you say in it?
Francie:	I put "Who Lost What in the Central Station last night?". Good, eh Josie?
Josie:	You're liable to get a' kinds o' funny answers to *that*. Anyway, let's have a dekko at the wallet.
Francie:	Sure . . . There you are . . .
Josie:	Mm . . . this must-a cost a few quid itsel'. Well, hello 'rer . . . he should be very grateful to get this lot back. The question is, *how* grateful? Ten per cent?
Francie:	Oh, I don't know Josie. Ye see, my Auntie Jessie always says that "Honesty is it's *own* reward".
Josie:	Aye . . . well, it wasnie your Auntie Jessie that found it, so whit do *you* say?
Francie:	Ten per cent!
Josie:	Right . . .
Francie:	*Plus* the money it cost me to phone the telegram.
Josie:	Fra-ancie, in a deal o' this magnitude, a few pennies are neither here nor there . . .
Francie:	Josie, my Auntie Jessie *also* says, "If you look

after the pennies the pounds'll take care o' themselves!".

Josie: Did she never tell you that "Empty vessels make the most sound"?

Francie: Naw . . . but she warned me that "A bird in the hand is worth two in the bush".

Josie: We-ell, when it comes to "birds" . . . I'd sooner take my chance in the bushes! Right, I think we are agreed that if we return this money intact, we shall both receive a substantial "bung".

Francie: Should do . . .

Josie: Francie, you will notice I said "Return the money *intact* –"?

Francie: Aye . . .

Josie: Every pound . . . every shillin' . . . every *penny*.

Francie: Josie! I wasnie thinkin' o' spendin' any o' it!

Josie: Naw . . . but *I* was. So . . . we shall place it out of temptations way.

Francie: How?

Josie: We'll bank it.

Francie: Aw Josie, I've always wanted to have a bank account – let's put it in my name, eh Josie?

Josie: We-ell, a' right . . . seein' as you found it.

Francie: Smashin'! Y'know somethin'? I've never even been in a bank before. I'd better get my clean socks doon off the pulley.

Josie: Fra-ancie, nobody in the bank'll ever notice yer socks.

Francie: Josie, they will if I *don't* change them!

Josie: Oh . . . ! Much d'ye say was in here?

Francie:	A hundred an' thirty five quid!
	Josie counts the money. When they get to the bank the teller examines the notes very carefully indeed.
Teller:	It's the first time I've seen the Queen's head upside down! They're all forgeries!
Josie:	Now wait a minute, we know whit you're thinkin' but it's nothin' to do wi' us . . .
Francie:	It's no' even our money!
Teller:	I'll have to inform the manager – this is a matter for the police!

Francie & Josie: The Police!

Francie: Josie, whit will we do?

Josie: Don't lose the heid Francie . . . DO NOT PANIC! This calls for clear thinkin' . . . there's only one thing to do –

Francie: Whit Josie?

Josie: RUN!!!!

THE BIRDS

Francie & Josie and a Pair of Au Pairs

Francie & Josie are on a train at night and they're wearing cheap imitation Panama hats and carrying guitars. In a quiet compartment, two Danish girls are asleep.

Josie: Francie, this is ridiculous! We've come the whole length o' the train – might as well o' *walked* to Glesca and saved the fare.

Francie: Josie, ye know I like a compartment to mysel'. I hate a' they folk sittin' lookin' at ye as if ye had horns on. (Francie checks another compartment to see if it's empty.) Ach, there's two young, smashin' lookin birds got in there before us . . .

Josie: Yer hard to please. Aw, hold on . . . *two young, smashin' lookin' birds???* Ya idjit!!

Francie: I saw them first Josie – !

Josie: Aw, they're awf'y nice . . .

Francie: I told ye they were smashers . . .

Josie: To sleep, perchance to dream. Whether 'tis nobler in the mind to tiptoe quietly oot o' here *or* to stay an' chat them up? That is the question Francie.

Francie: And we know the answer Josie . . .
Hedy & Ingrid stir when the door slams shut. Hedy is the first to realise they are not alone.

Hedy: Oh – ! (nudges Ingrid)

Ingrid: Mm . . . ?

Hedy: We have company . . .

Ingrid: Oh – !

Josie: (Removing hat with a flourish) Good evening
            ladies.

Francie: (Hastily doffs hat) How do ye do?

Hedy & Ingrid: Good evening.

Josie: I trust that we has not alarmed youse by our
            sudden and I hope not unpleasant mani-
            festations?

Hedy: Please, our English is poor – we not understand
            quite.

Francie: I not understand quite mysel'.

Josie: So . . . you're foreign birds – I mean, yer no'
            British?

Ingrid: No, we are Danish.

Josie: Of course – *Danish* . . . it's written all over ye! But
            er . . . tourists usually come earlier in the year –
            during our summer.

Francie: Aye, ye should have been here in July – we had
            a lovely day one Sunday.

Hedy: We are not tourists – we are au pair girls.

Francie: Au pair?

Josie: Aw pair-a stoaters if ye ask me.

Hedy: We come over and live with Scottish families
            and they give us food and a little pocket money.
            In return we, er . . . help with the housework but
            mainly we look after the children.

Francie: Oh, that's nice. Here, maybe ye could come to
            my house.

Hedy: Oh, you have children?

Francie: No-o .... but I could get some! There's a lot of them hangin' about the streets naebody seems to want.

Josie: Francie, are you tryin' to start up another Dr. Barnado's Home?

Francie: Not fancy the idea Josie?

Josie: I fancy the idea all right but *not* the way you put it.

Ingrid: We are all . . . arranged, with Glasgow families in eh'm . . .

Hedy: Ke-el – vin – side?

Francie: Oh, Kelvinside!

Hedy: It is nice, er . . district?

Josie: Ye-es . . . we-ell, it's got big houses, big cars . . . big heids! There's just one thing puzzles me. Why don't you just do this kin'a job back home?

Ingrid: We come here to-to . . . improve our English.

Josie: (Sarcastically) Oh, you'll definitely improve yer English in Glasgow.

Hedy: Six months we are studying – meeting the peoples . . . becoming with them er . . . how you say – intimate?

Josie: I think the word you want is familiar.

Hedy: Ah, yes! You think it possible that Glasgow peoples will becoming familiar to us?

Francie: Possible –? It's highly likely!

Josie: Well now, considering what you has just told us, it is very fortunate that we, er . . . run across each other. You want to mix wi' people an' we're

55

	people – aren't we Francie?
Francie:	Well, er . . . . ye-es.
Josie:	Er . . . I should like to make a small suggestion. Perhaps me an' Francie could help ye wi' yer English. After all, what yiz read in books is all very well but we can learn ye the common language.
Francie:	Aye, common is whit we speak.
Ingrid:	It is very kind of you –
Hedy:	But it makes for you er . . . a lot of trouble.
Josie:	Not at all, only too delighted.
Hedy:	Maybe Ingrid and I could teach *you* something?
Josie:	Could be . . . could be!
Hedy:	Are you knowing anything about Denmark?
Francie:	Denmark! Of course – ye make smashin' bu'er.
Josie:	Francie, you do not say "bu'er" – it is butter.
Francie:	Oh – ! . . . sorry. Butter.
Josie:	That's be'er. Now let's see . . . Denmark – yes! As I remember it, Hamlet was a great Dane.
Francie:	And Josie should know – he used to have a job doon at the kennels.
Josie:	Hamlet was a Prince, Francie. Lived in a big castle up there at Elsie-snores. He used to take a stagger roon the battlements every night . . . chattin' away tae his aul' man. 'Course, actually his aul' man was deid.
Francie:	And naebody had telt him he was deid Josie!
Josie:	He knew he was deid. It's just that he got more intelligent conversation oot o' him than I'm gettin' out o' you.

Francie:	I must say, I find it all very confusing Josie.
Josie:	Well, I have to admit I found it all very confusing too an' I sat through the picture twice, wi' big Lizzie McIntyre – that wid confuse anybody. However, that's another subject er . . . Where do ye think we are Francie?
Francie:	Eh . . . I think we're just about Cambuslang.
Josie:	Well, another ten minutes an' we'll be in Glasgow.
Hedy:	Ten minutes! If you will please excuse, we will go and make ourselves fresh.
Francie:	We'll just stay as we are, we're fresh enough.

The girls leave the compartment.

	Well, we lost the Go-As-You-Please competition Josie but it looks as though we've won the consolation prize.
Josie:	Ye-es . . . got to play our cards right though – these is no' ordinary birds.
Francie:	No Josie.
Josie:	They expect us to further their education.
Francie:	*Yes* Josie.
Josie:	So we'll invite them up to the house, parse a few sentences . . .
Francie:	Eh – ? Aye . . .
Josie:	Then we shall have a meal by candlelight in the backroom followed by dancing to sweet music played on your Auntie Jessie's pornograph.
Francie:	Aye Josie . . .
Josie:	That way they will see that us Glaswegians is used to high living.

Francie: Couldnie be any higher Josie – we're three stairs
           up in a tenement!

*Francie & Josie often had a message for their loyal fans
which they delivered at the start of their legendary
stage performances . . .*

A MESSIDGE FROM
FRANCIE & JOSIE

(Dictatit by Josie and writ doon by Francie)

Ladies and gents (to use an expression of convenience),

Many of youse here the night will no doubt experience a thrill of pressure as we make our very first exit before you, for we have perspired the-gether to make a spectacle of wursels by foisting upon a expectorant public an outstanding shower of incredible nonentities, all of who has been steeped in the rancid legend of showbusiness since early puerility right up to the age of adultery.

With their unbridled talent, truss and support, it will be wur endevvir for to present before your very eyes a work which for sheer hypocrisy and slite-of-hand will live for never in the annuals of all maternity.

Eyes will bulge and perspiration will roll as wur residential dancers and singers make spectacles of themselves before youse. These dancers are haun-picked (and we know whose haun it WIS!) for their beatitude, stamina and ableness for to move quick. (Something that Francie and me has first-haun experience of.) The costumes that the lassies wear costs as much as £750 a square yard, which seems a waste of dosh since they never wear any more than a fiver's worth.

We must pay tribune to wur producer, Jamie Phillips, who sews the costumes by haun – sometimes while the burd is actually in it. Also our director and corryographer (so-called because he is left-handed), Dougie Squires. Dougie is a most popular and skilful exponent of the art of The Dancin', being the winner of the Fandango Competition at the Drumchapel Arts Festival in 1937. Dougie has often been compared to Gene Kelly – mainly because he was a dancer as well.

We would like to extend wur thanks to the management of the Kings Theatre for giving us this work, and in particular for their endevvirs to get rid of the woodworm in the balcony.

Tea will not be served during the second interval mainly because there isnae one, and also in vue of the fact that we have lost the tea bag.

We hope most perversly that youse enjoy yoursels the night, cos Francie and me likes nothing worse than to see folk suffer.

Yours faithfully,
Francie & Josie

P.S. Please excuse pencil.

GIVE 'EM A JOKE!

A FEW OF FRANCIE & JOSIE'S FAVOURITES . . .

THE D.H.S.S.

Francie: (Menacingly) NEXT! How-can-Ah-help-ye?

Josie: Ah'm gonnae be a single parent.

Francie: You look mair like a single fish.

Josie: How dare you. Ah've never been spoken to like that in ma life.

Francie: Away! Have ye never been up in the Housin' Department?

THE POLIS

Josie: Yes, missus, can I help ye?

Francie: Yes, Ah want tae report ma man missin'.

Josie: Your husband's missing. Right. How long's he been missing?

Francie: Well, he came home for his tea last Friday, washed himself all over, and just went clean away.

Josie: Right. Give me his description.

Francie: Well, he's six-feet-two, blond hair, blue eyes, athletic, muscular build . . .

Josie: Wait a minute, wait a minute. Ah know your husband. He's five-feet-one, baldy head, watery eys, and weighs a ton . . .

Francie: Uch, Ah know THAT – but who the hell wants HIM back?

AT THE BUS STOP

Josie: Haw, Sandra, Ah huvnae saw ye fur ages.

Francie: Naw. Ah've no' been well.

Josie: Oh? Whit's up wi' ye?

Francie: Ah cannae breathe right.

Josie: Ye cannae breathe right? An' have ye seen aboot it?

Francie: Oh aye. Ah've been under the doctor a' week.

Josie: Oh, Goad. Nae wonder ye cannae breathe right.

THE AMERICAN TOURIST

Josie: (American) Say, pardon me for asking, but is that a hole you're digging in the middle of the highway?

Francie: Naw, the budgie died, so Ah'm buryin it!

Josie: Oh, yeah, very droll. And tell me, what is that thing you're leaning on?

Francie: This is ma shovel.

Josie: A SHOVEL! Why, Lordy Lord, back home in the States we got TEA SPOONS bigger'n that.

Francie: Ah'm no' surprised. Wi' the size o' yer mooth ye'd NEED it!

THE GLASGOW TAXIS

Josie: (American) Taxi! Hey TAXI!

Francie: Hello there, sir. Where to?

Josie: D'you know Loch Lomond.

Francie: (Rubbing his hands) Indeed I do, sir.

Josie: Well sing it to me while you drive me to Central Station.

Francie: There ye are, sir. Central Station. That'll be a hundred and four pound sixty.

Josie: From HOPE Street?

Francie: That's right, sir.

Josie: You think I'm stoopid, don't you? You think I'm just a dumb American. Well, listen, Smart Guy, you can't fool me. I did this same journey yesterday and it only cost me ninety-eight-fifty!

THE AMERICAN AND THE KILT MAKER

Josie: Say, bud, can I buy a kilt here?

Francie: Indeed you can, sir. Any particular tartan?

Josie: Well, I dunno. Can I wear any tartan I want to?

Francie: Of course you can, sir. Now here's a lovely material. Makes up very well. And as you can see, it's absolutely waterproof.

Josie: And such a lovely bright YELLOW colour, too. What tartan is it? A Hunting Stewart?

Francie: Er – no – actually it's a Cycling Mackintosh.

ARNOTT'S

Francie: Good morning, missus, can I help you?

Josie: Good morning. I want half-a-dozen invisible hair nets, please.

Francie: Invisible hairnets. Certainly, missus. Here we are.

Josie: Are you sure these are invisible?

Francie: They're no' hauf, missus. We've been oot o' them for three weeks, and Ah've been sellin' them a' mornin'!

THE BUTCHER'S

Francie: Good morning.

Josie: Good morning, madam.

Francie: I'd like some loin chops, please, and would you make them LEAN!

Josie: Certainly, madam, to the right or to the left?

BAYNE AND DUCKETT'S

Francie: Well, I'm sorry, missus. Ah've hud nearly every shoe box in the shop open, and ye don't seem to see anythin' ye want.

Josie: Well, ye see, it's actually not for me. I'm really looking for a friend.

Francie: Oh, well, come on let's open the last box. SHE MUST BE IN THAT YIN!

HONEY, HONEY

Francie: Good morning, how may I help you?

Josie: Ony Honey?

Francie: Naw, honey ony.

CROCODILE SHOES

Francie: Good morning.

Josie: Good morning. Can I help you?

Francie: Yes, I'd like some crocodile shoes, please.

Josie: Certainly. What size does yer crocodile take?

BRASSIERRY

Francie: Good morning, madam. What can I do for you?

Josie: Ah want a brassierry.

Francie: Certainly, madam. What bust?

Josie: Nothin' bust. It just wore oot.

Francie: No, you don't understand, madam. I mean size. What size do you take?

Josie: Oh. Ah take a forty-two cup.

Francie: FORTY-TWO! My God thy cup runneth over.

A WEE LIST

Francie: Ding, ding. Good morning.

Josie: Good morning.

Francie: I'd like some groceries, please.

Josie: Groceries. Certainly. Have you got a list?

Francie: Naw, it's just the wey Ah'm staunin'.

PUMP

Josie's Mother & her World-famous Pumping

Josie has just finished playing the piano.

Francie: That was marvellous, Josie. Very cultured. Just
right for this kinna joint, dump – er – theatre. Ye
see, people forget how cultured you and me is –
are! An' Ah'd forgotten how – er – well ye play.
Did ye enjoy it yourself?

Josie: Oh, aye. Ah always enjoy a good rummle on the
piana. 'Tho, mind ye, Ah had a wee bit trouble
wi' ma arpeggio there.

Francie: Aye, well there ye are. As ma mother always
used tae say tae me "you should have went
before ye sat doon".

Josie: Naw, naw. An arpeggio is where ye run up and
doon and then go intae a crescendo.

Francie: That's what Ah'm sayin', Josie. Ye should have
went before ye sat doon. But listen, you come
from a musical family, d'ye no'?

Josie: Oh, Ah do that. Ma father wis a rare singer. Hud
a lovely voice.

Francie: And wis he trained?

Josie: Naw, but he wis clean aboot the hoose. An' ma
sister wis a virtuoso.

Francie: Yes! An' havin' met yer sister, Ah cannae say
Ah'm surprised. Am Ah no' right in thinkin' she
hud a lotta trouble wi' a French Horn.

Josie: That is correct. But eventually she got it a'
            straightened oot.

Francie: Aye, Ah remember. Thon wis the longest
            trumpet Ah've ever seen in ma life. But it wis
            your father and mother that were so
            marvellous, Josie. Every Sunday in church, eh?

Josie: Oh, whit a double act, eh. Ma father played the
            organ and ma mother pumped for him.

Francie: Oh, lovely. And whit a terrific pumper yer
            mother wis, eh Josie?

Josie: Oh, naebody could pump like ma mother
            pumped.

Francie: Well, AH'VE never heard anybody pump like
            your mother pumped.

Josie: Oh, people came from far and near when they
            heard ma mother was gonnae pump.

Francie: They did. Ah'm surprised they didnae stay
            away!

Josie: Oh, whit a pumper. It jist seemed tae come
            naturally to her. Of course, she'd been pumpin'
            on and off for forty years.

Francie: Aye. When your mother pumped, Josie,
            everybody knew about it.

Josie: But whit a tragedy, eh? Mind thon Sunday?

Francie: Oh, don't, Josie. Ah cannae bear it.

Josie: Whit a way tae go. Right in the middle o' a
            pump!

Francie: It musta been the best pump she's ever done.

Josie: There she wis, pumpin' away good style, an' –
            an' – her lever broke.

67

Francie: Aye. Jist came away in her hand.
Josie: Aye. Not that it bothered HER, but it certainly
           put the wind up ma faither.

A TAP ON THE HEID

Francie: Er – Josie, Ah'm sorry tae butt in, but could I ask you something. It's very important.

Josie: Whit?

Francie: Have you got night starvation?

Josie: Nuttatall. It's only members o' the government that get that.

Francie: Well, Josie, I've got it. And d'you remember that pimple I got.

Josie: Where?

Francie: On ma holidays. Well Ah wis a wee bit worried about it. Ah thought it was mair than a simple pimple, ye know. Ah thought maybe it was something serious like a plook, ye know. And another thing, Ah get terrible nightmares.

Josie: Ach, Ah've dreamt aboot workin' an' a'.

Francie: Josie, it's not about work I dream. It's food. See last night – all night long Ah dreamt Ah wis eatin' spaghetti. Eatin' spaghetti all night. And when Ah woke up this mornin' . . .

Josie: Whit?

Francie: Nae cord on ma pyjama troosers. So I went tae the doctor and he gave me a wee rummle over wi' his periscope.

Josie: And whit did the doctor say?

Francie: Oh, he was quite definite. He said I had water

69

on the brain.

Josie: Away, your brain dried up years ago.

Francie: No, Josie. That's what he said. Watter on the brain. Now what would you do for a thing like that?

Josie: Try a tap on the heid.

Francie: Josie, Ah'm sorry to keep on about this, but how would you get a tap into my heid?

Josie: Aw, Francie it's simple. They'd take ye intae Gartnavel, give ye a local anaesthetic . . .

Francie: A *whit*?

Josie: A local anaesthetic . . .

Francie: Never in your Auntie Nelly. If I'm having an operation, I'm going to Bon Secours and I want twilight sleep!

Josie: Away for Heaven's sake. They don't do that any more. Anyway, twilight sleep is only for labour.

Francie: There ye are, Josie, that's what wrong with this country. Everything's labour. There's nothing for the Conservatives. Anyway there's no point in thinking about it. I mean, if I go into hospital who's going to keep the house clean.

Josie: Whit are ye talkin' about? The hoose couldnae get much dirtier. Did you know it wis the mice that sent for the sanitary?

Francie: That's not true, Josie. You know that my Aunty Jessie comes up regularly and keeps the house clean.

Josie: Yer Aunty Jessie? Whit did she do the other day there? Rinsed oot a milk bottle. Emptied the

	ashes oot the dresser drawer – intae the bureau drawer. Then swept a' the muck under the bed.
Francie:	Well, we always sweep the muck under the bed.
Josie:	Aye, but now it's gettin' serious. When Ah got oot ma bed this mornin' Ah bumped ma heid on the ceilin'.
Francie:	Well, here's a suggestion. Supposing we got a wumman in tae clean the house, and my Aunty Jessie could devote all her time to nursing me.
Josie:	Aye, Ah thought ye were gonnae say that. Look whit happened the last time yer Aunty Jessie wis nursin' you – when ye had the jaundice. Mind when ye had the yella jaundice?
Francie:	I had the yellow jaundice.
Josie:	Aye, and there ye were lyin' in the kitchen bed a' newly decorated in sunshine yella. An' yer Aunty Jessie comes up and pits ye intae a pair o' yella pyjamas.
Francie:	Well, whit aboot it?
Josie:	Whit aboot it? We couldnae find ye for three days.
Francie:	Is that what was wrong, Josie. Ah noticed ye pass two or three times an' ye never looked at me. Ah thought ye weren't speakin'.
Josie:	Ah didnae see ye. Yer Aunty Jessie knows nothin' aboot illness. Look at that time she was ill hersel'.
Francie:	She was very ill.
Josie:	She was nothin' of the kind. She went tae the doctor an' he said there wis nothin' much wrong

wi' her. A' she hud wis a MINOR virus.

Francie: A minor virus.

Josie: A minor virus. She wis gonnae sue him.

Francie: How?

Josie: She said she's never been near a pit-heid in her life.

THE NURSES

Francie & Josie appear as nurses Florence and Edith and open with a take on the classic song 'Sisters'.

Both: Sisters! Sisters!
Rushin' round the wards with kidney bowls and bedside pans,
God help you, mister,
If YOU should get ME or my sister,
And God help you, sister,
If WE get you into our hands.

Francie: Well, how's it gaun, Florence?

Josie: Uch, no' too bad, Edith. Ah wis glad tae get the exams over, were you no'? How'd ye do?

Francie: Aw, kinna eaksy-peaksy. Ah mean didnae mind the writin'-doon bit, but Ah wisnae havin' them lookin' in ma mooth.

Josie: Whit are ye talkin' about?

Francie: The oral examination.

Josie: Naw, naw. It doesnae mean lookin' in yer mooth. It means answerin' questions wi' yer mooth. It wis easy. They asked me whit acute bile wis.

Francie: And whit is it?

Josie: A fly cuppa tea. 'Course Ah've got a natural

73

	bent for this job.
Francie:	Aye, Ah've seen ye bendin'.
Josie:	Naw, Ah mean Ah've always wanted tae be a nurse. Ever since Ah wis a wee girl helpin' ma daddy wi' the blood transfusions and the bandagin'.
Francie:	Oh, wis he a doctor?
Josie:	Naw, a hairdresser!
Francie:	Well, anyway, that's the exams over. And here we are – CERTIFIED! Here, Ah meant tae say tae ye, did ye see Desmond Wilcox in the ward the other day? He wis lookin' for some nurses for a television programme all aboot the GRIM FACTS O' NURSIN'.
Josie:	Oh, are ye in it?
Francie:	Naw, he said the programme wisnae THAT grim. Mr. Kerr, the new surgeon's in it. Stoater, in't he. Know this, if it wisnae fur the specs and the moustache, he wid be the spittin' image o' ma mother, wouldn't he?
Josie:	He husnae GOT a moustache.
Francie:	Naw, but ma mother has.
Josie:	Ah hud dinner with him on Friday.
Francie:	Naw!
Josie:	Aye, we're havin' what ye call an "appendicitis romance". Ah grumbled that much he hud tae take me oot.
Francie:	Oh, he's nice. An' he's awfu' good wi' the patients. Especially in the operatin' theatre. Keeps them a' in stitches.

Josie: He gave me a set of angora underwear for ma burthday.

Francie: Oh, were ye pleased?

Josie: Tickled pink. You still gaun wi' yer toy boy?

Francie: The medical student? Oh, aye. He's graduated now, of course. He's a doctor.

Josie: Oh, does that mean you're gonnae get married right away?

Francie: No, no. He'll want tae practice for a few years first.

Josie: Ye didnae enter for the Personality Contest the other week.

Francie: Naw, whit was a' that about?

Josie: Och, it wis the Nurses' Committee that started the idea. See, we got this particular patient, and the nurse who could give him the highest temperature was the winner. Ah wis disqualified!

Francie: Whit, ye mean . . . ?

Josie: Naw, naw! He died o' hypothermia. Mind you Ah didnae like bein' on that committee. See that Ina McBangle – she's only the TREASURER cos she's got the biggest PURSE. And Bessie McDiarmid's only the TREASURER cos she's got the biggest BIRO.

Francie: And whit are you?

Josie: Ah'm the chairman!

Francie: Ah'm on night duty next week. Hate it. Ah mean ye just don't know what to do tae pass the time, do ye? Ah thought of a couple o' things . . .

	like wakenin' the patients at three o'clock in the morning tae ask them if they were sleepin' alright. Though what a stramash we hud wan night. We hud a V.I.P. in the ward.
Josie:	A V.I.P.?
Francie:	Aye, a vulture in plaster. Started complainin' tae me that there wis somebody nibblin' the chocolate in his locker. Ah says, well, don't look at me, Ah says – it'll be a moose. Oh, he says, a moose is it. Well, he says, it must be a gey clever moose, it's away wi' ma libery book an' a'. And, know whit he did? He set a trap for it in his locker. A MOOSETRAP! . . . AND WHIT A HAND AH HAD!!!!!!!
Josie:	Oh, Ah know. Ah wis on the casuallity last week. And we hud a fella in there – wan of the most serious cases of shock known to medical science. Apparently his wife said she was gonnae leave him, and didnae.
Francie:	Oh, Ah've hud them, too. Ah hud a fella come in tae ask if we could do something about the nasty gash on his mother-in-law's face. Ha-ha! It wis her mooth!
Josie:	Aye. Then there's the phone calls. Wan man phoned me up. Help, he says. Oh, help. Ma wee boy's just swalleyed ma ball-point pen. Ah says, don't panic, Ah says. Haud on. The ambulence'll be right there. Whit are ye doin' in the meantime. He says, Usin' a pincil!
Francie:	The things we've got tae put up wi', eh? Did ye

	hear aboot auld Mrs. Ramsay?
Josie:	Whit aboot her?
Francie:	Well, ye know she aye sleeps wi' her mooth open.
Josie:	And whit a mooth.
Francie:	Oh, yon's a cavity and a hauf. Well, the other week Ah'm on night duty. She's lyin' there, mooth wide open and giein' her adenoids laldy – when suddenly she screams.
Josie:	Oh, whit wis up?
Francie:	She'd swalleyed a moose.
Josie:	Oh, my. Wis it the same wan that hud been at the fella's chocolate?
Francie:	Aye. NAW! This was a REAL moose. Anyway, Ah didnae know just what to do. Ah mean, it's no' every day a thing like that comes up. So Ah got a haud o' the big Tom Cat. And Ah pit a bit o' CHEESE on Mrs. Ramsay's chin. The idea bein' that when the moose came up tae get the cheese, the cat wid nab it.
Josie:	Any good?
Francie:	Swalleyed the cat!
Josie:	Oh, Ah never liked the casuality. Know ma favourite? The labour ward. Though why they called it the labour ward Ah've never understood. As far as Ah could see not wan o' the patients wis the least bit interested in politics. 'Course on the other haun' if ye get yersel' pregnant, ye cannae be a' that conservative!

Francie: Aye. See that Mr. Stewart's wife's pregnant again.

Josie: Naw! An' that's him wi' the bad back!

Francie: Aye. This is their ninth wean. NINE WEANS! Ah mean, ye wonder where they get names for a' these weans. Ah asked her the other day. Ah says, whit are ye gonnae call THIS wan. She says, Ah'm callin' this wan Quits!

Josie: Did ye hear about Big Ina up there?

Francie: Big Ina?

Josie: Aye, her they call Big Ina Chology. This fella comes up tae see his new born baby – an' he wouldnae accept it. Oh, he says, Ah'm no' havin' that, he says. There's something far wrong here, he says, that's no' normal. He says, Ah want that replaced immediately, he says, it's a' wrang, he says. Then we discovered Big Ina wis haudin' it upside doon. Ah must say Ah wondered – Ah mean Ah thought it had an awfu' big grin on its face.

Francie: Och, she's as blind as a bat, you yin. On a clear day she can just see her glasses. Mind thon wumman that wis all upset cos she thought her baby had pure white hair. Then we discovered Big Ina wis pittin' the talcum on the wrang end!

Josie: Aye, Ah wonder anybody ever comes back tae this hospital. Mind thon day you an' me were left in the casuality a' by wursel's?

Francie: Oh, wis thon no a scream?

Josie: Suddenly these fifteen fellas came in an' we

didnae know whit tae do wi' them.

Francie: You speak for yersel'.

Josie: Oh my – An' Ah telt them jist tae take off a' their clothes an' staun in a line. Did ye ever see anythin' like yon. Fifteen grown men staunin' there in the scud.

Francie: Aye. Just hingin' aboot.

Josie: They were that embarrassed. Didnae know whit tae do wi' their hauns. They kinna missed their pockets.

Francie: An' thon wee fellah wis annoyed, wisn't he? Oh, he wis annoyed. You could tell by his face. He says, Ah don't know whit the hell ye've got me like this for, Ah'm only here fur an ingrowin' toenail.

Josie: Aye, an' the fella next tae him says, you can talk he says, Ah only came in tae clean the windaes!

Both: God help you mister,
If YOU should get ME or my sister,
And God help you sister,
If we get you intae our hands.

LE BISTRO MANQUE

FRANCIE & JOSIE AND THE ENTENTE CORDIALE

The boys reminisce about their trip to Paris and an awfy nice lassie fae Dennistoun . . .

Francie: Mind *we* were in London, Josie.

Josie: That's right. Last year.

Francie: Aye, on wur way tae Paris when *they* were the City of Cultyer.

Josie: Aye.

Francie: Celebratin' their bicentenary.

Josie: Aye.

Francie: Josie, whit are ye celebratin' when ye're celebratin' a bicentenary?

Josie: Oh, it's an old Rid Indian custom. They used tae celebrate a bicentenary every time they'd shot two hundred bison. Paris wis brilliant, though, wintit?

Francie: Oh, the berries. Especially the food. Cordon Blue!

Josie: Cordon Blue? Awaaaaaaay! You think Cordon Blue is when ye're hemmed in by the polis. Oh, but see Paris!

Francie: See thon nightclub.

Josie: See the lassies dancin'.

Francie: Can can!

Josie: Wish Ah could–could!

In Montparnasse, Paris, the proprietor of a typical French bar is talking to a very sexy lady called Gabrielle who is dressed Apache-style. There are men everywhere in various stages of intoxication and dancing girls enter doing the can-can. Francie & Josie arrive to survey the scene.

Josie: There ye are, Francie. Whit d'ye think of it?

Francie: Aw, it's terrific, Josie. Terrific. It could be the Griffin Bar.

Josie: (Spotting Gabrielle) Oh, jings, would ye look at that!!! Now THAT is what ye call a piece-de-resistance!

Francie: Whit's a piece-de-resistance?

Josie: That's a French burd that wants ye tae buy her dinner first.

Francie: By jings, Ah think Ah know her, Josie.

Josie: Ye know her?

Francie: Aye, is that no' the Madonna wi' the big boobies?

Proprietor: Allo', allo'!

Francie: There, whit did Ah tell ye!

Proprietor: (With strong, garlicky breath) 'ow can I 'elp you?

Josie: Ye can stop breathin' for a start.

Francie: My God, has he been eatin' auld insoles?

Josie: Naw, it's the garlic, Francie.

Francie: Oh, Ah beg your pardon. Ochone, Ochee. Kimerra hashie. Kimerra how. Slanjay var.

Josie: Ah said GARLIC, Francie, no' GAELIC!

Proprietor: You are Eengleesh?

Francie: Whit d'ye think we should do, Josie?

Josie: Well, speakin' personally . . . Ah think . . . Ah'm
            gonnae huvtae hit him in the mooth.

Francie: Naw, Josie, stay cool. Use yer diplomacy.

Josie: Aye, yer right, Francie. I will say this only the
            wance, masseur. We happen tae be Scottish.
            Scottish, ye understand? And you, I take it are a
            dirty great Froggy schmuck?

Proprietor: (Nodding happily) Oui, m'sieur, Oui!

Josie: (Still smiling and nodding) Ye've a breath on ye
            like rancid kippers!

Proprietor: (Delighted) Merci, m'sieur, merci. You are
            Scotteesh. I like Scotteesh. I 'ave a cousin who
            leeves in Scoatland.

Francie: Naw, whereaboots?

Proprietor: Edinburgh.

Francie: Aw, jings, nae wonder ye've bad breath.

Proprietor: You would like a table, Messieurs? What
            about thees table 'ere?

Josie: Oh, well, it's no' that we're clannish nor nuthin',
            but we don't fancy sittin' wi' Kinnock and
            Hattersley there. Can we no' have a table tae
            wurselves?

Proprietor: A table of your own, messieurs, a table you
            shall 'ave.
            He picks up a bottle and hits the men over the head. They
            fall to the floor and are carried away by the waiters.

Josie: Now, that's what I call service, Francie.

Francie: Aye. They could be doin' wi' somethin' like that
            at the DHSS.

82

Proprietor: Now, messieurs, what about something to drink? You would like something really superb? Wat if I say to you – Peena Colada?

Josie: I couldnae do that tae ANYBODY'S colada! Naw, je tell ye whit, masseur. Avvy voo ony VP?

Francie: Here, that's marvellous, Josie. Ah didnae know ye could speak French.

Josie: Ach, it's nothin', Francie. Listen tae this. Eh, masseur. Avvy voo the time the noo?

Proprietor: Oui, oui!

Josie: Naw, naw. That's avvy voo the LOO the noo. Ach, never mind. Jist donnay us oon bottle o' yer best bevy. Okay? And some sangwidges if ye've got them.

Proprietor: Le sandwich, oui, m'sieu.

Francie: That is marvellous, Josie. Where did ye pick up the lingo?

Josie: Ach, well, Ah used tae knock aboot wi' a French polisher.

A man wearing a dirty raincoat and a beret appears and approaches furtively.

Beret: Pssssssssst. Pssssssst. Pssssssssst.

Francie: WHO is?

Beret: Psssssst! Pssssssst!

Josie: D'you smell gas?

Beret: M'sieu.

Francie: AAAAAAAAH! Who, me?

Beret offers some postcards.

Beret: Oui, m'sieu. You like to buy naughty French postcards? Very French – very naughty. Look . . .

Josie:	(Eyes popping) In – the – name – o' – God! Here, have ye any in Cinemascope? We're kinna broad minded.
Francie:	Let's see it, Josie. Ah could maybe send one tae Auntie Jessie.
Francie:	Oh NAW!
Josie:	Whit's up, Francie?
Francie:	That *is* ma Auntie Jessie.
	Francie shoves the postcards back at Beret.
Beret:	Very well, m'sieu. You no' like postcards. Perhaps you like the ladies' stocking, ah? Very nice. Very French. See they have the lovely leetle message. Read, m'sieu.
Francie:	(Reads) No matter how long the stocking is, the top is always nearest the bottom!
	They all laugh.
Josie:	(Freezes) Ah don't get that!
Francie:	Ach, Josie. No thanks, china.
Beret:	Well, what about some perfume, m'sieu? So sexy. Smell! Eet ees called ECSTASY.
Francie:	(Sniffing it) Oh, by jings, that's ECSTASY alright. It smells like a fish supper.
Beret:	Eet weel recall the moment when you lost all control and gave way totally to your animal instincts.
Josie:	Aye, ye're right enough. It smells like recycled lager. Here. Lager off.
Beret:	But, m'sieu . . .
Francie:	Listen, is that a drum ye've got in yer ear?
Beret:	Oui, m'sieu.

Francie: Well, beat it.
             The Proprietor arrives back with champagne, glasses and some little sandwiches.
Proprietor: Is thees one bothering you, messieurs? I will feex heem. Attendez. Attendez.
             He calls over his henchmen and the vendor is dragged away screaming.
Josie: Er . . . now, ye're no' gonnae . . .
Proprietor: Worry not, m'sieu. He will seemply be invited to take a bath. In the Seine. Now, messieurs. 'Ere we have eet. Champagne and caviar sandwiches. The best in the house.
Francie: Er, Josie, can we afford this . . . ?
Josie: Caviar, eh? Very nice.
             He takes one, chews and ponders.
Josie: (To Francie) It's fish fingers.
Proprietor: If there is anything else, m'sieu, do not hesitate to call.
Josie: Aye, well, listen Ah tell ye what – give all yer pals a drink. Champagne all round.
Proprietor: Oh, merci, m'sieu. You are very kind. (Calling) Champagne for everyone. Thees kind gentleman is paying.
             There are calls of 'Merci' and 'Très bien'. The Proprietor goes and Josie pours the champagne.
Francie: Er, Josie . . .
Josie: Cheers, Francie! Just look at this champagne – see the sparkle, see the bubble. Look oot, stomach, here comes trouble.
Francie: Josie! Are you sure we can PAY for this?

Josie:	Francie, stop worryin'. Have Ah ever let ye down?
Francie:	(Unravelling his red, checked napkin) Er, Josie. He's gi'en me Yasser Arrafat's headdress. Whit's this fur?
Josie:	Honest tae God, Francie, Ah can take ye naeplace. Ye can be a right ignorant nyuck sometimes.
Josie:	This is whit the yuckies cry a SERVIETTE. They use it tae wipe their mooths instead o' their sleeves. Ye see, this'll maybe come as a terrific surprise tae you, Francie, but some folk eat affa PLATES. No' like us that nearly always eat oot a newspaper.
Francie:	Well, Ah've seen folk in Kelvinside eatin' oot a newspaper.
Josie:	Aye, maybe ye have, but Ah'll bet it wis the *Glasgow Herald*. Anyway, tae get back tae the serviette. When yer friends in Kelvinside sit doon tae their dinner they've always got wan o' these. Ye see, they can cover a multitudinous array of mishaps. Let me give ye an EG. Supposin' yer sittin' there havin' yer dinner. The first thing ye do is take the serviette and open it up, just like a big hanky. Then, hauding same between the thumb and forefinger of the right haun, ye ram it doon yer thrapple – so! Now you're sittin' there when suddenly, to your utter bereavement – ye rift. Well, if it's a dry rift, ye just turn tae the fella sittin' next tae ye and gi'e him a dirty look. However, should the rift not be

dry, but in so doing you have covered your chin wi' mince . . . right? Well, you take the serviette between the thumb and first finger of the right haun', so! And, very carefully, wipe the mince aff yer chin – so. Taking very great care to fold the serviette IN the way – so that ye come tae a clean daud for the next time!

They tuck in to the sandwiches and champagne. Gabrielle approaches, puts one long leg up on the table and smoothes her stocking. The boys are dumb-struck.

Francie: Josie!

Josie: Whit?

Francie: Don't look now, but Ah think Avon just called. D'ye think she's tryin' tae attract our attention?

Josie: If she is, she's going the right way about it. Well, what are ye waitin' for?

Francie: Ah'm waitin' tae see what happens when she puts her other leg up.

Gabby: Do you mind if I join you?

Josie: Why? D'ye think we're comin' apart? Ha ha ha! Just a very small joke.

Gabby: (Seating herself) Yes, I'm surprised it was allowed out by itself. I am Gabby.

Josie: (Smarting at the insult) Ye're no' hauf!

Francie: Would ye like some champagne, Gabby?

Gabby: Yes, thank you, but I have Dom Perignon waiting for me at the bar.

Francie: Well, maybe he'd like some champagne as well?

Josie: Francie, Dom Perignon *is* champagne. Allow

me, Gabby. Garcon, encore de champagne, mais maintainant, une bouteille de Dom Perignon.

Proprietor: Oui, m'sieu. I know what Gabby likes.

Josie: Vous ette un dirty old homme.

Francie: Ye furra sangwich, Gabby?

Gabby takes one but Francie fumbles the plate and drops a sandwich on the floor. He goes to pick it up but is stopped by Josie.

Josie: Don't you dare pick food up aff the flair.

Gabby: Tell me, what part of France do you come from?

Francie: Oh, we're no' fae France. We're fae Glasgow.

Gabby: (In a broad Glasgow accent) NAW! Whit part?

Josie: Coocaddens!

Gabby: Dennistoun!

Josie: (Delighted) NAW!

Josie: (To the bar) Oh, this calls for a celebration. Garcon, more champagne. More champagne for everybody.

Proprietor: Oui, m'sieu. Thank you, m'sieu.

Francie: Hey, Josie, how are we gonnae pay for this? The dole money's no gonnae cover a' this.

Josie: Trust me, Francie. Just trust me.

Gabby: I just love champagne, don't you?

Josie: At home, we drink it like Irn Bru.

Francie: That *is* Irn Bru, Josie.

Gabby: I like the way it tickles your nose. Does it tickle *your* nose?

Josie: Naw, no' really. But then, I always drink it through the mooth. Here, Gabby, Ah've got a great idea. What about the three of us goin' oot the night? We'll have a slap-up dinner and then go on the town.

Francie: Josie, the money. Where do we get the money?

Gabby: Terrific. Ah'm just gonna do a wee number now, but Ah'll be with ye in aboot ten minutes after that. Gonnae keep ma place!

Francie: Josie. The money. We cannae pay for a' this.

Josie: Don't worry, Francie. It'll be alright.

Francie: Have they still got the Bastille here?

Josie: Ach, you worry too much. It'll be good for the entente cordiale.

Francie: Whit's lime juice got to do wi' it?

Josie: God help us. Entente cordiale isnae lime juice.

Francie: Well, whit is it, then?

Josie: Well, it's a . . . a . . . a kinna . . . sometimes there's a certain . . . where a lotta people gather . . . Maybe it *is* lime juice.

Proprietor: Ladies and gentlemen, the lovely – GABRIELLE.

There is applause and Gabby and a male dancer start to perform an Apache dance. As the dance progresses, however, Francie & Josie take exception to the way that Gabrielle is apparently being molested.

Francie: Hey, Josie. Did you see that?

Josie: Hey, watch it, you. That's our china.

Francie: Aye, ye better watch it. She's fae Dennistoun.

Another apparent assault.

Josie: Hey, did you hear me? Leave that burd alone or you'll have tae make do with the wan nostril.

Another assault and this time Francie & Josie move

in and get to grips with the male dancer. He pushes them away and tries to get on with the dance. They bring the Apache down and he crawls under the curtain, only to be grabbed again and thrown into the pit. Pandemonium follows.

Gabby: (Grabbing them) Come on, run like the clappers.

Proprietor: (Stopping them) One moment, messieurs. Haven't we forgotten something?

Josie: Aye, we have. A previous engagement.
            The Proprietor signals and the three of them are surrounded by henchmen.

Proprietor: There is a little matter of three thousand, seven hundred francs, m'sieu.

Josie: Three thousand, seven . . . Oh, as – er – mu – as lit – is that all?

Francie: (Beginning to cry) Oh, Josie, Ah told ye . . . What are we gonnae do? It's you and me for the guillotine.

Josie: Francie, shut yer face while I'm doin' business. Let's see now. Three thousand, seven hundred francs. That's aboot, roughly, four hundred quid. Ach, look, call it four-fifty. There ye go. Okay?
            He thrusts a bundle of coupons into the Proprietor's hand and they make to go, but are stopped.

Proprietor: A moment, m'sieu. What are these?

Josie: These? That's the new British pound.

Proprietor: (Nodding his head in satisfaction) Oh, the new British pound? Est bien.

Josie: Aye. See it there. B.P. – British pound.

Francie: By jings, that was a near thing, Josie.

Josie: Nuttatall! Ah told ye these petrol coupons would come in handy one day . . .

CULTYER

Josie: Thank you. Thank you most securely. It is with
            the most heartfelt temerity that we join with you
            in saying how good it is for you to see us again.
            I see all the cognochanties and intelligenitals are
            with us the night. And that you are sitting there
            in a welter of expectoration. So we trust that
            wur ambivalence the-night will be meretricious
            to all concerned. Int that right, Francie?

Francie: Oh, sure, Josie. Sure Josie, sure, sure, sure!

Josie: We are especially delightful to be here during
            Glasgow's year of culture. Cos, let's face it,
            when it comes tae culture – we know a thing or
            two, eh Francie?

Francie: By jings, no' hauf, Josie. See Francie and Josie,
            see culture! We're certainly . . . Whit exactly *is*
            culture, Josie?

Josie: Isn't that funny. Pat Lally wis askin' me that
            very thing only the other day.

Francie: And whit *is* it?

Josie: Well, it's a' the finer things in life. Like opera
            and drama and paintin'. Ah mean, take Michael
            Angelo. Ye know Michael Angelo.

Francie: Aye, sure. He's got the chip shop at Kelvin
            Bridge.

Josie: Naw, naw. Michael Angelo – fifteenth, sixteenth

century. He wis a very famous artist. He was also the first DIY man.

Francie: Wis he, Josie?

Josie: Aye. Paintit his own ceilin'. An' when the Pope saw it, he decided tae make a gesture.

Francie: (Hesitantly showing two fingers) Whit, ye mean . . . ?

Josie: Naw! The Pope widnae do THAT! He might do THAT – but no' THAT! He commissioned Michael Angelo tae build his tomb. However the poor old Pope didnae live tae enjoy it. He died afore it wis feenished.

Francie: So whit did they do?

Josie: Just went tae Wylie and Lochheid like everybody else. But there's a veritable cornucopia of culturial delights in Glasgow EVERY year. For instance – look at the Burrell Collection.

Francie: Oh, Ah love them. Especially the dark wans wi' the soft centres.

Josie: Whit are you talkin' about?

Francie: Burrell's chocolates. Smashin'!

Josie: That's BIRREL. Ah'm talkin' about BURRELL.

Francie: Well, whit kinna sweeties dae THEY make?

Josie: They don't make sweeties. It's a kinna museum in Pollok.

Francie: It's a hoose in Linthaugh Road!

Josie: Nuttatall. Some o' the stuff is hundreds o' years old.

Francie: That's Linthaugh Road!

Josie: Ye don't understand. They're anticues worth thoosands o' pounds. For example, there's Roddin's Thinker.

Francie: Roddin's THINKER? And whit's he thinkin' about?

Josie: He's thinkin' about how tae get oot o' Pollok. How the hell should AH know? It's no' a fella. It's a statue.

Francie: Oh, a telephone.

Josie: A whit?

Francie: A telephone. Hello, sta-tue!

Josie: Aw, forget it. Let's try ballet. Noo, we've SAW a ballet, haven't we?

Francie: We have saw a ballet, Josie.

Josie: Giselle!

Francie: Aye, an' HE's no' up tae much, either.

Josie: That wis the name o' the ballet. Mind thon wee wumman wi' the net mini-skirt, an' thon fella wi' the white tights. By God he wis big, thon fella, wint' he, Francie?

Francie: (Remembering) Oh, God, aye. He wis big!

Josie: A big, big fella!

Francie: He wisnae just BIG – he wis SHUGE!

Josie: He wis big.

Francie: Musta been at least six-feet-four!

Josie: Aye, he wis tall as well! Speakin' of big fellas Ah went tae see big Robbie Coltrane in his "BUFFO".

Francie: Whit – wis he in the scud?

Josie: Nuttatall. Robbie Coltrane wouldnae stoop that low.

Francie:	Robbie Coltrane COULDNAE stoop that low!
Josie:	Listen, Francie, Mistero Buffo wis pure culture. There wis nae scud. It wis a wan-man-show wi' Robbie Coltrane playin' a' the parts himsel'.
Francie:	Ah'm no' surprised. Wi' Robbie Coltrane on stage there wid be nae ROOM for other actors.
Josie:	Actually, Ah've met Robbie. An' ye know, he's a nice big fella. And ye'll mebbe find this hard tae believe, but he's quite a shy bloke. Ye know, doesnae have a lot tae say for himself – doesnae mind bein' on his own – doesnae have many friends.
Francie:	Kinna like a Scottish Conservative.
Josie:	What culture is REALLY about is the PEOPLE. The City and the people who live in it. Mind you, there's some rotten folk that live in EVERY city. Thieves and vagabonds and con-merchants.
Francie:	Now, Josie, that's no way tae speak about Glasgow District Cooncil.
Josie:	Ah'm no' talkin' aboot the cooncil. Ah'm talkin' aboot the hard men; the lager-louts, an' the thieves an' murderers.
Francie:	Och, them. Know whit I would do, Josie? Ah would put them on a big boat an' sail them away tae some island miles away; pit them aff an' let them get on wi' it.
Josie:	Ach, they tried that years ago, an' look whit it brought us.
Francie:	Whit?

Josie: *Neighbours*. But Glasgow is really lookin' super these days. An' it's got such terrific architecture. Ah mean, see the municipal buildin's.

Francie: Ach, Ah'm no' sure Ah like that place. A' these tiled walls an' corridors. Feels like a big public lavvy.

Josie: Well, why d'ye think they call it the City Chambers? Naw, it's a great place. All Ah want tae know is – now that Nelson Mandela's oota jail can we go back tae callin' it St. George's Place? But, ye see, Glasgow has been famous for so many things. Architecture, shipbuildin', medicine, exploration . . . Did you know it wis a Glasgow man that discovered a herd of rare snow-white pigeons. These pigeons were actually breeded by two different tribes in South America called the Incas and the Dincas.

Francie: And what were the pigeons called, Josie?

Josie: The Inca-Dinca Doos.

Francie: Josie, ye know it all, eh? But, listen, Ah'll tell ye about explorin'. Ye know that big glass-frontit buildin' in Albion Street?

Josie: The *Glasgow Herald* office, aye.

Francie: Aye, but it's NO' the *Glasgow Herald* office. No' many people know this, but that big glass-frontit buildin' in Albion Street is really – a LAVVY!

Josie: A LAVVY! Aw, come on, Francie. Ah'm no' just as stupit as you give me credit for.

Francie: Ah'm tellin' ye. Aboot twinty year ago there wis a famous explorer in Glasgow called A.E. Pickard. Ye mind o' A.E. Pickard?

Josie: Aye. He used tae have a lotta old bangers up wan side of his driveway.

Francie: That's right. And a lotta old motor cars up the other. Well, he told me the story himself. He went oot tae the Himalayas tae try and catch a Yeti.

Josie: A YETI? Whit the hell's a Yeti?

Francie: It's a great big ferocious thing wi' a flat face and a straggly fur coat.

Josie: Away – that's your Auntie Jessie.

Francie: Naw, it's no'. It's a Yeti. Whit they call an Abominable Snowman. It's a great big thing aboot twenty-five feet tall.

Josie: Whit, bigger than the ballet dancer?

Francie: MILES bigger! Anyway they caught wan and brought it back to Glasgow and they kept it in the old Union Cold Storage Company that used tae be in George Street, so that it could live in something like its natural habbiatat. Then they discovered they hud a problem.

Josie: Whit kinna problem?

Francie: A BIG problem. There wis nae lavvy!

Josie: Nae lavvy fur the Yeti?

Francie: Nae lavvy fur the Yeti. At least no' wan that wis big enough. So they BUILT wan. And that is the glass-frontit buildin' in Albion Street.

Josie: AWAY! Are you tryin' tae tell me that the *Glasgow Herald* buildin' – a NEWSPAPER office is a lavvy for an Abominable Snowman? Ah gave ye credit for havin' mair sense, Francie. Somebody's been pullin' yer leg.

Francie: Aw, naw, they huvnae. Ah'm no' stupit, Josie. Ah checked it out, right. Ah stood there an' watched wan day – an' AH SAW THE ROLLS O' PAPER GOIN' IN!

PURE NEURALGIA

FRANCIE & JOSIE AND THE BURDS AND THE BEES

Josie: Thank you most peculiarly, Chinas. That was the most wonderfullest deception, for which I thank you from the bottom of my heart – and of course, Francie's bottom also. Speaking of which, I know you will be interestit to hear that Strathclyde Uni were keen to make Francie a Doctor of Arts. Unfortunately, he didnae hear it right and turned it doon. Anyway, may I just say how delightful we are to have this opper-chancity of exposing wurselves to you wunce again. Int that right, Francie.

Francie: Oh, sure Josie. Sure, Josie. Sure. Sure. Sure.

Josie: That wis some greetin', wintit?

Francie: Magic, Josie. Jist magic!

Josie: It's a big difference from the greetin' we got the first time we appeared in this theatre, wintit?

Francie: Oh, no' half, Josie. There wis only two folk came tae see us an' we were a' greetin'. But all that changed when they pit us on the telly, didn't it?

Josie: Oh aye. That wis away back in the Sixties. By jings, the Sixties were amazin', weren't they, Francie?

Francie: Oh, pure neuralgia, Josie. Pure neuralgia.

Josie: Er – that's nostalgia, Francie. Neuralgia's a kinna pain in the neck.

Francie:	That's what Ah'm sayin', Josie. Pure neuralgia!
Josie:	How? Did you no' like the Sixties?
Francie:	Ach, they were alright, but the way those Teddy Boys used tae dress was embarrassin'.
Josie:	Aye, true enough. And the hair-dos they hud. Never hud their hair cut. Jist went in fur an oil change.
Francie:	Aye. Remember the wan that went intae the barber and hud 'is hair cut wi' a parting right across his heid this way – fae ear tae ear.
Josie:	And whit happened tae 'im?
Francie:	Ach, he scrubbed it. He got fed up wi' folk whisperin' up 'is nose.
Josie:	Aye. 'Course we were never Teddy Boys. We were the TONY Boys. The suits WE wear are cut in the ITALIAN style like what we saw in the Italian Riviarea.
Francie:	Aye – Largs! Oh, Josie, mind the Hot-Pea-Specials in Largs? An' the fish suppers in the wee cardboard boxes tae keep the grease aff the haudin'-haun' . . . An' remember the night we went intae Nardini's . . . AN' SAT INSIDE! An' – an' – Josie, it wis YOU that introduced me tae coffee wi' Drumaderry sugar. It wis the first time Ah'd ever hud it.
Josie:	Hud whit?
Francie:	Coffee wi' Drummaderry sugar.
Josie:	Oh, aye? Did ye have wan hump or TWO? On the other hand, Francie, it wis YOU that introduced ME tae CHINESE FOOD. Mind we

	took a coupla burds tae the Chinese restaurant?
Francie:	Aye, an' you got cauld feet and settled furra fish supper.
Josie:	Aye, an' then Ah asked the wee Chinese waiter fur the salt an' pepper.
Francie:	Aye. An' the waiter pit wan haun in his poakit, an' he says, YOU WANN SALL? Then he pits 'is haun' in 'is OTHER poakit, an' he says YOU WANN PEPPAH?
Josie:	Oh aye. Thank God Ah didnae ask fur the vinegar!!!!
Francie:	Oh, it was a magic, romantic night wi' those burds. Candlelight, a yung-chow-fried-rice, an' a gin-and-Persil tae clean oot yer mooth. Tell me, Josie, why do we always refer tae girls as 'BURDS'? Ah mean Rabbie always talked about 'lassies' – why do we call them 'BURDS?'
Josie:	Aw, Francie. We went through a' that years ago in primary school. D'ye no' mind when the teacher was givin' us lessons aboot sex? Remember?
Francie:	Oh aye Ah remember the sex lessons a'right, but it wis a' jist THEORY!
Josie:	Aye, Well Ah think that's as far as ye're supposed tae go in Primary 3. But d'ye no' remember she told us all about THE BURDS AND THE BEES. Mind she explained that the girls were BURDS and the boys were BEES.
Francie:	Oh aye, Ah think Ah remember that. The burds and the bees.

Josie:	Aye, and Ah remember you got a wee bit confused about the birds and the bees, didn't ye?
Francie:	Naw.
Josie:	Aye, ye did. Whit did ye do the first time ye took a lassie tae the pictures?
Francie:	Och, Josie.
Josie:	Go on, tell us.
Francie:	Ah took 'er a boxa worms.
Josie:	A boxa worms!
Francie:	Uch, Josie. Ah wouldnae huv brought that up.
Josie:	Naw, but SHE did!
Francie:	Anyway, nobody can say Ah don't know about the burds and the bees now!
Josie:	Oh, Ah'm no' so sure about that. Ye wurnae a' that keen on the wee burd you met in Largs.
Francie:	Wee Sandra?
Josie:	Wis that 'er name – SANDRA? Goad, every Tom, Dick and Harry's ca'ed Sandra.
Francie:	Aye, Sandra. She wis a'right.
Josie:	A'right???! She wis eighteen!
Francie:	That's right. Jist eighteen.
Josie:	Eighteen stones in weight! She wis the fattest wee barra Ah've seen in a long time.
Francie:	Oh aye, she wis fat, but she wis approachable.
Josie:	Aye. From every angle. Did you know she couldnae wear elastic roon her knickers?
Francie:	What did she huv, then?
Josie:	Swish Rail! Anyway, they werenae as good as the Glasgow burds. Look at the burds we used

	tae get at the dancin'.
Francie:	Aye, right enough, they hud class, the Glasgow burds. Mind how ye always hud tae wait for them at the Ladies while they got their coats.
Josie:	An' she would hand over her dancin' pumps fur you tae carry for her.
Francie:	Aye, an' ye could always tell whereabouts she lived by the newspaper they were wrapped in.
Josie:	Aye. It wis a bit embarrassin' tho', wintit, carryin' the pumps in newspaper? Ah always used tae carry them very carefully in wan haun', an' blow on them so's folk would think it wis a fish supper.
Francie:	And mind when we got them tae their tenement, we used tae get them up against the wall in the back-close for a snoggin' session. My God, ye could hear it echoin' up an' doon the close.
Josie:	Naw, Ah never done that. Ah wis more interestit in 'er mind.
Francie:	(Looking at him in bewilderment) Her mind? Whit's 'er mind got tae do wi' it? Are you tryin' tae tell me you never got anythin' up the back close?
Josie:	'Course Ah did.
Francie:	What?
Josie:	Measles! Anyway, there's more tae life than big sookers up a close. Ah like tae discuss important issues wi' people; talk about the meanin' of life an' that. Ah think it's important for human bein's tae pass things on tae wan another.

Francie:	Ah, well, that burd fairly passed it on when she gi'ed you the measles.
Josie:	There ye are, ye see, there's no point talkin' tae you. Your heid contains nothin' but an impenetrable wall of superfluous bone matter.
Francie:	Oh! And whit does THAT mean?
Josie:	It means (tapping his head) the hoose upstairs is tae let. The truth is, Francie, you are seriously lackin' in cultyur.
Francie:	Aw, CULTYER, CULTYER. Ye're always on about CULTYER.
Josie:	Well, culture is very important. You ask Pat Lally. Have you read Shakespeare?
Francie:	Naw!
Josie:	Have ye read Dickens?
Francie:	Naw!
Josie:	Well, whit huv ye read?
Francie:	Ah've red pyjamas.
Josie:	I am nutt desirious of discussin' your aprez-curry raiment. I am talkin' about BOOKS. Ye know whit a book is!
Francie:	Aye. That's fur bettin' on the gee-gees.
Josie:	It's nothin' o' the kind. A book is a collection of small dauds o' paper stuck the-gither at wan end.
Francie:	Och, THAT?! Aye, Ah've got wan o' them at home.
Josie:	Oh, an' whit's it called?
Francie:	Andrex.
Josie:	Francie, I regret fur tae tell you this, but there's

only wan way tae describe you and that is ILLITERATE.

Francie: I beg your pardon, Josie, my father and mother were . . .

Josie: Ah'm no' talkin' about yer father and mother. I am talkin' about litteratteraterature. What dae you know about Scott's works?

Francie: Scott's works? Whit dae they MAKE?

Josie: Whit do they make, he says. Scott's works. Whit dae Scott's works make?

Francie: Well, what DO they make?

Josie: PORAGE OATS, OF COURSE!

SWEET VIOLETS

A FRANCIE & JOSIE FAVOURITE

Sweet violets,
Sweeter than the roses.
Covered all over from head to toe,
Covered all over with sweet violets.

There was a young miner who worked down the pits,
Who fancied a girl who had fabulous – earrings,
And lived with her folks in Lochgelly.
The neighbours all noticed she had a big – garden,
Although they were really quite poor.
One of the residents called her a – sweetheart,
The way she looked after her folk.
Her father was mingin', he'd give ye the –
Sweet violets, etc.

The farmer she worked for was quite thrilled to bits,
Cos just like the miner, he'd noticed her – earrings.
And trained her to run his farm-STEAD.
The farmer was eager to get her to – like him,
And put her in charge like a fool.
Cos one day he found she'd been milking the – profits,
And made herself really quite rich.
He called her a strumpet, he called her a –
Sweet violet, etc.

The next day the farmer was all teeth and smiles,
Explained he got angry because he had – problems,
And asked if she'd like to be kissed.
The young girl refused cos she knew he was – puggled.
He sacked her and called for a taxi,
She told him to shove his job right up his – jumper,
Because she was happy to quit,
She belted him one and he fell in the –
Sweet violets, etc.

And so she returned to the boy in Lochgelly,
And offered her love and her rather large – bank book,
The young miner knelt to propose,
Then went out and bought her a ring for her – finger,
And with it he offered his heart,
She got so excited she let off a – firework,
To celebrate THEIR *wedding day,*
From that day to this they have rolled in the –
Sweet violets, etc.

WEE ARRA PEOPLE

A GLASGOW HISTORY LESSON

Josie: Ye know, Francie, Glasgow is an amazin' city.
          Just the other day Ah wis walkin' down West
          George Street through Nelson Mandela Place –
          intae Pat Lally Street – up through the Idi Amin
          Necropolis – and Ah wis thinkin' tae maself:
          there are buildin's in Glasgow that would take
          yer breath away.

Francie: What, ye mean like the Fishmarket?

Josie: NAW! Ah'm talkin' about the beautiful old
          established buildin's we've got. Ah mean, it's
          nae wonder Glasgow's been defecatit the City of
          Architecture. An' there's gonnae be some terrific
          new buildin' for the year Two Thousand. What
          dae YOU think they should do for the
          Millenium?

Francie: Ach, Ah don't think we should bother wi' the
          millenium, Josie. Ah mean, naebody *plays* it
          these days.

Josie: Have you ever thought of huvin' a lo-botomy?

Francie: Whit's a low-bottomy?

Josie: It's an operation ye get tae jack up yer
          bahoochie. Ye know how, as some people get
          older, their bums kinna slide doon underneath
          them, and they start walkin' as if they were
          sittin' doon! Big Sandy McGrouther's hud it

	done. Unfortunately they jacked it up too high and noo he's walkin' aboot wi' a hump. Naw, there's gonnae be a lotta super things for the Millenium. For example, George Square is gonnae be turned intae a beautiful cemetery.
Francie:	Oh, good, Josie. That'll be the dead centre o' the City.
Josie:	Aye. That's where they're gonnae bury the toon cooncillors.
Francie:	When they die?
Josie:	Naw, right away. But when ye think what Glasgow's gonnae be like in the year two thousand, and ye think what it musta been like in the dim and distant past . . . Ye know, Ah read somewhere that five hundred thousand years ago, the estimated population of the whole of Scotland was only about *two hundred*. An' every wan wis a shop-steward. That's how the block vote came about.
Francie:	What's a 'block vote'?
Josie:	It means that only certain blocks hus the vote.
Francie:	(Greatly in awe) That's mind gobblin', Josie. An' that wis five hundred thousand years ago?
Josie:	Aye!
Francie:	(Posh voice) So under what circumstances was the city of Glasgow established, Josie?
Josie:	Ah, well, now that's an interestin' question . . . Hey, wis that you talkin'? Huv ye been goin' oot wi' somedy? Now, first of all the name "GLASGOW" comes from a couple o' celtic

	words meanin' *"THE DEAR GREEN PLACE"*.
Francie:	Ah. Parkheid!
Josie:	Nothin' tae do wi' Parkheid. The first settlers in Glasgow musta been the Ancient Britons.
Francie:	Whit, ye mean Barbara Cartland?
Josie:	Naw! The Ancient Britons were an off-shoot.
Francie:	She missed a penalty?
Josie:	Who?
Francie:	Barbara Cartland.
Josie:	Na-aw! It's got nothin' tae do with Barbara Bloody Cartland or the Celtic Football Club. Now listen. The first thing tae understand is the Roman invasion. They hud battered their way right up through England wi'oot any bother. And they got about a quarter of the way up Scotland when, suddenly, they were stopped dead in their tracks.
Francie:	Where wis this?
Josie:	Bearsden. They couldnae get intae Bearsden.
Francie:	How wis that, Josie?
Josie:	Well, THEY HUDNAE BEEN INVITED!!!! And can you see the Bearsden folk pittin' up wi' a loada fish suppers an' poky hats brought in by a buncha foreigners? So they sent for Lollius Urbicus, the Roman Governor of Britain, and he arrived in one forty one.
Francie:	Ooooh! The egit. Jist missed the beginnin' of 'Neighbours'.
Josie:	The year 141, ya nyuck. And he built a wall from the Clyde tae the Forth, and the Romans settled

	in furra long seige. Ye can still see the Wall. *Antonine's Wall* it's called. Then a Mysterious Monk arrived. He wis a Scottish monk –
Francie:	Fae Monklands.
Josie:	Aye. Naw. And he gathered a whole lotta other monks roonaboot 'im, an' they all took vows of chastisement.
Francie:	And whit does THAT mean, Josie?
Josie:	It means that SEX wis ANATHEMA to them.
Francie:	It gie'd them bronchitis.
Josie:	Ah said ANATHEMA no ASTHMA! It means they hud tae remain sellotape.
Francie:	And they were stuck wi' it!
Josie:	Aye. But, right away, the Mysterious Monk hud tae face a frightenin' problem. The plague wis spreadin' all over Europe.
Francie:	God, that Child Support Agency gets everywhere.
Josie:	Naw, naw. Ah'm talkin' about the real plague. They hud it in Edinburgh an' it wis awful.
Francie:	Whit, ye mean the Festival?
Josie:	Naw, it wis even worsen than that. Even worse than acne. Everybody wis stottin' aboot an' fallin' doon in the street.
Francie:	Away, that's no' a plague. That's Hogmanay in the Grassmarket.
Josie:	Anyway, happily, it didnae reach Glasgow. But, in the meantime, the Romans hud launched another attack. So they faxed the Mysterious Monk.

Francie:	Pardin'????!!!
Josie:	They sent a fax fae Bearsden tae tell 'im the Picts hud come doon fae the North and were harryin' the Romans.
Francie:	Harryin' them?
Josie:	Aye. Harry Thomson – Harry McNab – Harry Ramsden. They were a' there. But the Romans were winnin', so the Mysterious Monk ordered the Picts and the Bearsden folk tae dig great big holes in the road tae stop the Roman advance.
Francie:	And the holes are still there, Josie. All over the city. That's why Glasgow's called The Holy City.
Josie:	Exactly.
Francie:	But why were these Harrys from the North called Picts?
Josie:	Cos they picked their noses. Naw, that was the name the Romans gave them. It meant "paintit people" – cos they paintit wee arras all over their bodies. And ye know what they called themselves?
Francie:	What?
Josie:	WEE ARRA PEOPLE! But it didnae matter what they did, they couldnae get the Romans tae move. So the Mysterious Monk revealed hissel'. And ye know whit happened?
Francie:	He wis arrestit!
Josie:	Naw. The Mysterious Monk turned out tae be a well known and much loved monk called Sydney the Divine.
Francie:	And did HE get rid o' the Romans, Josie?

Josie: Aye. He sang tae them an' they ran like hell.

Francie: By jings that's some story, Josie. And isn't it amazin' that we can still see the Wall where all that happened. Ye know, Ah sometimes think that we get rid of too many old things that folk enjoyed. For example Ah loved the old Glasgow tram cars.

Josie: Oh the tram cars – me too, Francie. An' am Ah no' right in sayin' they're thinkin' o' bringin' them back?

Francie: Aye, but they're gonnae be great big long things. Ye get on at wan end, an' by the time ye get tae the other end ye're where ye're goin'.

Josie: Aye. An' they hud some really, really classic jokes, didn't they. It wis real typical Glasgow humour they told about the dear old trams.

Josie: Francie! Remember the wan about the sailor sittin' upstairs in the tramcar and some'dy asks 'im where he's gaun, an' he says "Well, as a matter of fact Ah'm gaun tae China, but thank God this is the worst o' ma journey over."

Francie: And, Josie, remember the one about the auld man sittin' gazin' oot the windae.

Josie: An' the conductor comes up tae 'im an' says, "Excuse me, sir, but your wife got off three stops ago."

Francie: And the auld man says, "Oh, thank God. Ah thought Ah'd gone DEAF!"

Josie: Then there wis the one about the fella that jumps on the tram an' says, "D'ye ... (stuttering) ... go tae – does this car go tae . . . . . . It's a'right Ah'm there!"

Francie: And this fella jumps on an' says, "How much is it tae Maryhill Road?" An' the conductor says, "It's fivepence tae Maryhill Road." So the fella jumps off and starts runnin' behind the tram. Then he jumps on again an' says, (panting a bit) "How much is it tae Maryhill Road NOW?" And the conductor says, "It's sevenpence now, ye're runnin' the wrang way."

Josie: Then there wis the wumman who wouldnae sit upstairs because there wis nae driver.

Francie: Aye, an' then there wis the big fat wumman that got on the tram when it wis full. Oh, she was BIG!

Josie: She was a big wumman!

Francie: She wisnae jist big, she wis HUGE. An' she says in a loud voice, "Is there not one single gentleman on this tram that'll get up and let a lady sit doon?"

Josie: Aye, an' wan wee fella got up an' says "Come on then, missus, Ah'll make a contribution!"

Francie: An' whit about the one about the poor old wumman that had been standin' fur ages in a crowded tram.

Josie: Oh, aye, an' this man complained tae the conductor an' said it wis a shame keepin' this poor auld woman standin' an' he should do somethin' about it.

Francie: That's right. So he pit her aff at the next stop!

Josie:	Oh, an' mind the one about the fella tryin' tae get on the tram wi' the dug? Here you, ye cannae get on the tram wi' that dug.
Francie:	How no'? It's a public convenience.
Josie:	I am in charge o' this vehickle, an' that animile is no' gettin' on the caur.
Francie:	But we'll go upstairs. The dug likes tae smoke.
Josie:	Ah don't care if he bursts intae flames, yer no' gettin' on this wi' that dug.
Francie:	But it's no' a dug, it's a whippet.
Josie:	Well, whippet tae hell aff the caur.
Francie:	Ah well, ye know whit ye can do wi' yer car.
Josie:	Aye, an' if ye'd done that wi' yer whippet, ye widda got OAN THE CAUR. By jings, they didnae half give the passengers a rough ride, eh?
Francie:	No' half. Remember the fella wi' this huge parcel on the seat beside 'im.
Josie:	Oh aye. An' the conductor says tae him, Heh you. Get that parcel affa that sate.
Francie:	Naw!
Josie:	Eh?! Are we deif or what, sir. You heard me. Get that parcel affa that sate.
Francie:	Naw!
Josie:	Listen you, if ye don't shift that parcel Ah'll fling it oot the windae.
Francie:	Oh aye, Ah'd like tae see ye.
Josie:	Alright. Have it your way. There, that's yer parcel oot the windae. What have ye got tae say tae that?

Francie:	Nothin' – it's no' ma parcel.
Josie:	Oh, an' Francie, what about the wan where this wumman comes on the bus wi' her son. Remember? One and a heff, please.
Francie:	Aw come on, missus. Ye cannae get half fare fur a boy that size. He's sixteen if he's a day.
Josie:	Ay beg your pardon, Aive only been merried thirteen years.
Francie:	Listen missus, Ah'm here tae collect fares no' confessions.
Josie:	Ay beg your pardon, Ay hev never been so insulted.
Francie:	Away. Huv ye never been tae the Housin' Department? Come on, this boy's wearin' long troosers. Ye cannae get half fare if ye're wearin' long troosers. Ye only get hauf fare if you're wearing short pants.
Josie:	Oh, well. In thet case *I'LL* take the heff.
Francie:	An' the wee wumman sittin' opposite said, "Here, if that's the way ye work it, Ah'm due ma money back."
	Oh an', Josie. D'ye know ma favourite.
Josie:	Whit?
Francie:	There's this big Hielanman comes on the tram an' he asks fur a tuppeny wan. An' the conductor says tae, "a'right," he says, "but ye'll huv tae pay for yer dug." An' the big Hielanman says, "Whit ye talkin' about? That's no' a dug – that's ma sporran." An' a wee wumman leans forward an' says, "D'you know," she says, "Ah

wondered about that. Ah offered it a biscuit an'
it widnae take it."

DANCE HALL PATTER

FRANCIE & JOSIE ON PULLING BURDS

Josie: Ye know, Francie, thinkin' aboot the hysteria of Edinburgh, d'ye mind the nights we hud at the Fountainbridge Palais?

Francie: Aw, those were the good old days, Josie. The young folk nowadays don't know how tae dance.

Josie: Naw. In OUR day the fellas used tae keep a haud o' their burds. Nooadays, they just staun an' waggle away by themselves. Sometimes they end up wi' some four-eyed tart they've never seen in their puff before.

Francie: Aye. An' they jist take them hame anyway.

Josie: That's right. We hud a kinna protocol in our day.

Francie: Oh, aye, Ah remember. Then ye went intae the shop the next day tae collect the picture.

Josie: I said PROTOCOL – no' PHOTOCALL.

Francie: Oh, sorry.

Josie: Naw, mind how the burds a' stood round the dance floor waitin' fur somebody tae dance them? And when ye wantit tae ask wan o' them tae dance ye went roon behind them an' tapped them on the elba.

Francie: (Doing it rather low down) Aye. D'ye fancy a dance?

Josie: Heh, watch it. That's no' her elba ye're tappin'.

Naw, the thing was they never looked at ye. They never turned round tae see who it wis.

Francie: Naw. Just walked straight on tae the floor, turned roon and pit her arms up ready tae go.

Josie: That's right. Mind we used tae go roon the back, tap them on the elba an' just staun' there. An' she went stottin' on tae the dance floor, turned roon wi' her arms in the air an' there wis naebody there. C'mon, let's do the Dance Hall Patter. For demonstration purposes only, you, china, will play the part of the burd.

Francie: Aw, naw, Josie. Ah'm no' bein' the burd. Ye always make me play the burd.

Josie: Cos ye do it that well. Look at a' that fan mail ye got when the fleet wis in.

Francie: Oh, aye, right enough. Awright, then. On ye go. *Francie stands a short distance away and poses, chewing gum and waggling his hips.*

Josie: Now, as you enter the dancing establishment, you will see that a' the spare burds is hingin' up against the wall. And as you can see – this yin's left her engine runnin'. Now, there is a formal approach which has to be made to the young female. Greetings, fair midden. I perceived that you were on your tod and wondered if you would care for a convolution or gyratory perambulation roon the hall?

Francie: Eh?

Josie: Are ye dancin'?

Francie: Are ye askin'?

Josie: Ah'm askin'!
Francie: Ah'm dancin'.
Josie: D'ye come here often?
Francie: Naw, just every night.
Josie: 'Sa rerr band, intit?
Francie: Aye, Ah just sent a request tae the drummer.
Josie: Oh? Whit did he say?
Francie: Beat it!
Josie: Anybody ever tell you ye danced like Cyd Charisse?
Francie: Naw!
Josie: Ah'm no' surprised.
Francie: Ah'll have you know dancin's in ma blood.
Josie: Pity it husnae got doon tae yer feet yit!
            Francie does "Hands in his Pockets".
Josie: Whit's that?
Francie: That's the Prince Philip.
            Francie does "The Hitch Hiker".
Josie: And whit's that?
Francie: That's "The Hitch Hiker."
            Josie does the "Trooser Bit".
Francie: Whit's that?
Josie: Troosers comin' down!
            They dance together.
Josie: 'Sa rerr flerr, intit?
Francie: Aye. Ah wish you'd get aff ma feet and try it fur yersel'!
Josie: Know somethin'? You're wan in a million!
Francie: So's yer chances!
            Josie's hands start to wander.

Francie:	Heh, heh, heh. Just you chuck that. Ah've only just met ye.
Josie:	Anybody seein' ye hame?
Francie:	Naw. Seein' masel' hame.
Josie:	Don't fancy yer job!
	Josie's hands start to wander again.
Francie:	Heh, Ah've warned you. Any more o' that an' Ah'll call for help.
Josie:	Ah don't need any help! But, c'mere, listen. Have ye no' got a lumber?
Francie:	Naw!
Josie:	Whaur d'ye stay?
Francie:	Balerno!
Josie:	Balerno!? It's no' a lumber you want it's a guide dog!
	Josie's hands start to wander yet again.
Francie:	Ah hud a different fella see me hame every night last week. That wis a feather in ma cap, wintit?
Josie:	Oh, definitely a feather in yer cap.
Francie:	An' Ah won the talent contest in the summer. That wis another feather in ma cap, wintit?
Josie:	Aye, aye. Definitely another feather.
Francie:	An' a won the Spot Waltz last night.
Josie:	Oh? How did ye manage that?
Francie:	Well, Ah hud mair spots than emdy else. But sure that wis another feather in ma cap.
Josie:	Och aye, for God's sake – it wis another feather.
	They stop dancing suddenly.
Francie:	Aw, heh, look at the time. Ah've missed ma last

bus. How Ah'm Ah gonnae get hame?

Josie: USE YER BLOODY FEATHERS AN' FLY HAME!

EMBRA

Francie: Tell me something, Josie. How did Edinburgh get its name?

Josie: Well now, that's an interestin' question. The name "Edinburgh" comes from a Gaelic phrase – Dun-eatin'.

Francie: Dun-eatin'.

Josie: Aye. The complete translation is "Come in – ye've hud yer tea, cos we've done eatin'." This is a very hysterical city, Francie. Everywhere ye go ye find hysteria. Did ye ever hear of Bloody Mary's Close?

Francie: Naw!

Josie: Well, Bloody Mary was actually a wumman called Mary King, who lived just off the High Street, right. Ye can still see the Close. Well, one day in 1645 – THE PLAGUE ARRIVED!

Francie: Whit, ye mean – ELDORADO?

Josie: Naw! Naw! It wisnae as bad as THAT. Naw, Ah'm talkin' about the REAL plague in 1645 when everybody was staggerin' about and fallin' down in the street.

Francie: Away, that's no' a plague. That's Hogmanay in the Grassmarket.

Josie: Nuttatall! This wis a disease. Even worse than acne. Everybody in the Close hud it. And ye know whit The Cooncil did tae stop it spreadin'?

Francie: Whit?

Josie: Well, they stapped up both ends, then they built the City Chambers right on tap o' them!

Francie: ON TAP O' THEM! Has Ian Lang done anythin' aboot this?

Josie: Course he hus. That's why he's ordered single-tier cooncils. Ye see, cooncillors were a bad lot in those days. D'ye know there wis one called Deacon Brodie that was hung fur bare-faced robbery.

Francie: Aye, well, some things never change.

Josie: But there wis a lotta GOOD folk there as well. The monks arrived in Holyrood Abbey aboot 1128.

Francie: Just in time for Prisoner Cell Block H at 11.30.

Josie: The YEAR 1128, ya banana. And of course bein' holy men they all hud tae take a vow of chastisement.

Francie: And whit does that mean, Josie?

Josie: It means that sex was anathema to them.

Francie: It gi'ed them bronchitis.

Josie: Naw it didnae. It means they hud tae remain sellotape.

Francie: Sellotape? Ah, well, they'd be stuck wi' it.

Josie: Aye. D'ye know it wis a monk that saved Scotland when the Romans invaded? They had stormed their way right through England wi'oot any bother. But they were stopped in their tracks at Cramond.

Francie: Did the folk in Cramond no' like the Romans, Josie?

Josie: Have you seen an ice cream shop in Cramond? Anyway the Romans built a wall right across Scotland from the Clyde tae the Forth. Then the Picts came doon and started tae harry them.

Francie: Harry them?

Josie: Aye. There wis Harry Thomson – Harry McNab – Harry Ramsden. And you shoulda seen the mess they made o' the Roman wall wi' their errasoles.

Francie: Their whit?

Josie: Their errasoles.

Francie: Ye mean they were sittin' on it?

Josie: Naw. ERRASOLE CANS! They were sprayin' slogans on the wall like "Tongs ya bas" and "Lisa loves Jacko" and "The gallery belongs tae Edinburgh." Then tae stop the Romans advancin' they dug great big holes in the roads.

Francie: Ah've seen them - Ah've seen them. The holes are still there.

Josie: That's right. And Glasgow copied them. They've got holes on ALL their roads.

Francie: Right! That's why they call Glasgow the Holy City.

HOLYROOD

FRANCIE & JOSIE AND THE GHOST OF RIZZIO

Josie: Ah must say they've made a lovely job o' the
            theatre. Amazin' what a lick o' Magicote can
            do?, intit?

Francie: Aye, but that's no' Magicote. That's Dulux. They
            got a big dug in tae do it.

Josie: Oh did they? Mind last Christmas we were
            appearin' at another theatre that wis jist newly
            paintit.

Francie: That's right. The Edinburgh Festival Theatre. It
            wis the same big dug.

Josie: Aye, Ah enjoyed that visit. We seemed tae get
            around more. Saw a lotta sights!

Francie: Aye, and most o' them were walkin' along
            Princes Street.

Josie: Know ma favourite place? The Scotch Whisky
            Heritage.

Francie: Oh, wonderful. Three days that took us.

Josie: Aye, we must go back an' see it wan day. Whit
            wis your favourite?

Francie: Aw, no contest, Josie. Definitely Holyrood
            Palace.

Josie: Ah, now that was really amazin'. Whit aboot
            Mary Queen o' Scots' bedroom?

Francie: As nice a bedroom as Ah've seen, Josie. Now,
            while we're on the subject, whit wis that big

plaque in the middle o' the flerr therr?

Josie: Oh that wis where Rizzio fell.

Francie: Jings, Ah'm no' surprised. Ah nearly tripped ower it masel'. Thon's dangerous, ye know. Somed'y could fall on their erky wi' yon, and mebbe contuse themselves.

Josie: Naw, naw. That plaque wis there tae commemorate events that took place in the sixteenth century.

Francie: The sixteenth century! By jings, eh! Wid that be A.D. or B.C.?

Josie: Ach, away and don't be stupit – they didnae have electricity in those days. Ye see, Rizzio wis an Italian and they murdered him.

Francie: Didnae fancy his ice-cream!

Josie: Naw, it wisnae that. Things jist seemed tae backfire on him.

Francie: Oh! Musta been his hot peas then.

Josie: Naw, ye don't seem tae understand. Listen, ye remember the bed?

Francie: A lovely bed, Josie.

Josie: Well, wan night Mary Queen o' Scots wis havin' a kip in that bed.

Francie: A kip?

Josie: Aye, a kip. A doss. She hud 'er heid doon.

Francie: Oh, aye. She'd taken a pill.

Josie: Away fur God's sake, the pill hudnae been invented then.

Francie: Well, whit did they use in those days?

Josie: Why d'ye think – they wore suits of armour!

Anyway, this night it was very dark. And the thunder wis rollin' across the skies, and wind was howlin', and the rain wis LASHIN' doon.

Francie: It wis Glasgow Fair Fortnight!

Josie: Naw, it wisnae. Anyway. Suddenly the door opened.

Francie: Eeeeeeeeeeek!

Josie: And Rizzio came in.

Francie: Wi' 'is oilcan!

Josie: He didnae have an oilcan. Rizzio came in an' they were a' waitin' fur 'im. An' they jumped on him. And stabbed 'im a' ower his back.

Francie: That wouldnae help his lumbago!

Josie: And there he lay. Totally deid. Stretched out in her chamber.

Francie: He wis a midget!

Josie: Naw he wisnae a midget. He wis a nutcase.

Francie: Ah! He wis a wee bit potty.

Josie: Anyway, ever since that day, the ghost of Rizzio has walked the corridors of Holyrood Palace. A desperate and dangerous spirit.

Francie: Buckfast!

Josie: Ah'm no' talkin' about that kinna spirit. Ah'm talkin' about GHOSTS!

Francie: Away fur Heaven's sake. Naebody believes in ghosts nowadays.

Josie: 'Course they do. Lots o' people believe in ghosts.

Francie: Who then, who? Tell me who!

Josie: Well, whit about yer spiritualists? They believe in ghosts.

Francie:	Do they?
Josie:	Certainly. Spiritualists believe in spirits and spirits is ghosts. Look at big Bella McGovern. She's a great spiritualist. She's aye gaun tae spiritualist meetin's. Bella McGovern goes tae a spiritualist meeting any time she's oot fur the messages.

Francie starts to laugh.

Francie:	Ha-ha-ha! That's a stoater. Every time she's oot fur the messages. Good, Josie.
Josie:	Whit ye laughin' at?
Francie:	What you said the now. Ye know – about Big Bella gaun tae a spiritualist meetin' any time she's oot fur the messages. Did ye no' mean tae say that? Ah thought ye meant tae say it. Ah jist thought it wis funny the way ye came oot wi' it.
Josie:	Came oot wi' what?
Francie:	What ye said the now. Ye know aboot Big Bella gaun tae a spiritualist meetin' any time she's oot fur the messages. Did ye no' mean tae say that? Ye know – MESSAGES – SPIRITUALIST MEETIN'!!!!! Ye know – when Bella goes tae a spiritualist meetin' she gets a message.
Josie:	Naw. Bella gets her messages fae Safeway.
Francie:	Aye, Ah know she gets her messages fae Safeway. But it wis just the way ye came oot wi' it. Ah thought ye were sayin' it fur a joke. Ye know how people go tae a spiritualist meeting tae get messages.
Josie:	Away and don't be stupid. Are you tryin' tae tell

	me people go tae a spiritualist meeting an' say "could I have a pun o' sausages please."
Francie:	They're KILOS now.
Josie:	Alright, are ye tryin' tae say people go to a Spiritualist meetin' and ask for a tin o' beans an' a pun o' KILOS?
Francie:	Naaaaaaw! Ah'm no' meanin' that. You said . . . You seemed to be sayin' that Bella . . . Naw, ye're right enough – it wisnae funny at all. Jist forget it. Go on wi' yer story.
Josie:	Well, this particular day Bella went tae a spiritualist meetin' tae see if she could get in touch wi' her dear departed husband, Wee Shuie. Well, they were all sittin' round this big table haudin' hauns in the dark, and the wee wumman that wis runnin' the meetin' started laughin'. Oh whit a state she wis in. Laugh, laugh, laugh.
Francie:	Whit was she laughin' at?
Josie:	She wisnae laughin' at anythin' in particular, she wis jist a happy medium. And suddenly – oot the dark – this trumpet came floatin' ower their heids.
Francie:	TRUMPET? Whit trumpet? Who ever heard of a trumpet at a spiritualist meetin'?
Josie:	Ye can have a trumpet if ye want it. It's voluntary. Anyway the trumpet floated doon tae the table, and suddenly it spoke. This wis Wee Shuie talkin' in B flat. An' Bella says, "Is that you, Shuie?" and Shuie says, "Aye, it's me,

Bella." And she says, "Are ye happy there?"
"Oh," he says, "it's marvellous here. The grass
is so green an' the sky's so blue, an' everythin's
so peaceful an' quiet." Bella says, "do ye like
bein' an angel in Heaven, Shuie?" "Oh," he says,
"Ah'm no' an angel in Heaven – Ah'm a coo in
a field in Whitletts."

Francie: I have never heard so much rubbish in all
ma life! A coo in a field in . . . WHO – WHO –
WHO . . .

Josie: D'ye stoap at Girvan?

Francie: WHO EVER HEARD OF ANYBODY COMIN'
BACK AS A COO!

Josie: 'Course people come back as coos. Where d'ye
think they get the reincarnation milk from!!!!!

THE ARBROATH GAG!

The Ultimate and Final Francie & Josie Gag

Francie: Come on now, Josie, time's gettin' on; it's time for the Big Finish. We've got tae go out wi' a bang. Ah tell ye what – tell them yer joke.

Josie: (Delighted) Oh, aye. Aye, Ah could . . . Whit joke?

Francie: Ye kno-ow! Thon joke Ah told ye. Ye've done it before. He tells this marvellous. He's told it on the telly an' everything. On ye go, Josie. Remember – the wan about ARBROATH!

Josie: (Beside himself) Oh, aye, ya beauty. (He roars with laughter at the thought but stops abruptly.) How does that go again?

Francie: Och, ye mind it fine. 'Member, there wis this chap at the door – an' this fella said "Is yer sister in?" On ye go.

Josie: Oh, aye. Ah remember. Ah remember. (He sets himself up.) There wis this chap at the door, ye see. An' when it wis opened, there wis this plumber.

Francie: WAIT A MINUTE! Ah didnae say anythin' about a PLUMBER.

Josie: Aye, ye did. You said there wis a chap at the door, an' this fella said "How's yer cistern?"

Francie: Ah didnae say ANYTHIN' about 'is cistern. Ah don't give a monkey's about 'is cistern. There

	wis a chap at the door, an' this fella said "Is your sister in?" SISTER IN. Nothin' tae do wi' a plumber.
Josie:	Oh, the plumber wisnae there?
Francie:	Naw. There wis nae plumber.
Josie:	(To the audience) I do apologise, I appear to have mizled you. It seems the plumber couldnae come that day.
Josie:	(Setting himself up again) There wis this chap – at the door. Ye see . . . An' he says, "parding me, but is your sister – in?" An' . . .
Francie:	Oh, wait a minute, Josie. That's wrong. It's ma fault, Ah'm sorry. It wisnae 'is SISTER.
Josie:	Wis 'is sister no' there either?
Francie:	Naw. The sister wisnae there.
Josie:	She's mebbe away lookin' for the plumber.
Francie:	Naw, wait, Ah've got it, now. It wis his GRANNY. That's it – there wis a chap at the door an' this fella says "Is yer granny in?"
Josie:	Is it alright if we go tae another street? Ah'm no' doin' too well here.
Francie:	Aye, on ye go. You've got it now. Oh, this is marvellous!
Josie:	(Setting himself up again) There wis this chap – at the door, ye see . . .
Francie:	Actually there wis TWO chaps at the door, but don't worry aboot it.
Josie:	TWO chaps?
Francie:	Aye, but it's no' important. On ye go.
Josie:	This fella knocked twice at this door . . .

Francie:	Naw he didnae. He only knocked ONCE!
Josie:	You just said there wis TWO CHAPS at the door.
Francie:	Well, so there wis, technically speakin'. There wis a chap that gave a chap at the door, and then there wis the chap that answered the chap that gi'ed the chap at the door.
Josie:	(Now totally confused) There wis a' these chaps at this door, an' they were lookin' for this fella's sister tae tell her her granny had run away wi' the plumber. An' this fella said, "well the last time Ah saw the plumber, he wis runnin' doon the street wi' a tin o' Harpic – Ah thought he wis gaun roon the bend . . ." So a' these chaps . . .
Francie:	WAIT A MINUTE!!!! Whit d'ye think ye're doin'? Ye're makin' a right pig's breakfast o' this joke. Ah don't know whit's the matter wi' you. You usually tells it that well. Now listen carefully, Josie. Ah'll tell ye jist wance more. This chap chapped at the door, an' he said tae the fella that answered the door "Is yer granny in?" And the other fella said, "Naw, she's at Arbroath." And the other fella said, "That's alright, Ah'll come in and wait 'til she's feenished!"
Josie:	Oh, aye. Aye, Ah remember – Ah've got it now. (He sets himself up yet again.) There wis chap at the door – ye see. An' this chap says, "Parding me, but has yer granny finished 'er soup yet?" An' the other chap says, "Naw, as a matter of fact we couldnae get the can open – we've loast

the tin opener." An' the other chap says, "Don't worry," he says, "Ah'm gaun tae Arbroath an' Ah'll pick wan up for ye on the way back."

Francie: (Screaming at him) Naaaaaw! That is rubbish. This chap's no' gaun tae Arbroath! He doesnae even know where Arbroath IS! He doesnae even CARE where it is. There's only wan person at Arbroath an' that's the granny. Keep that in yer heid. Granny Arbroath – Arbroath granny!

Josie: Sorry. Ah think maybe Ah confused ye there. It wis actually the GRANNY that had went tae ... Whit did she huv tae go tae Arbroath fur a plate o' soup fur?

Francie: She DIDNAE go tae Arbroath fur a plate o' soup. D'ye no' see – that's the joke – THERE WISNAE ANY SOUP!

Josie: Oh there wisnae ... Ah'm sorry, there's nae soup. Soup's aff. Naw, she's on the mince 'n' tatties noo. An' she likes mince cos it's hauf chowed before ye start. An' she's got everythin' there – big marrafat peas an' doughboys, an' the crinkly chips and sweet turnip – an' she's got big dauds o' white bread sookin' up the broon gravy, an' it's a' runnin' doon her chin and on tae her chemise ...

Francie: (Screaming again) Stoap it! Stoap it! You're makin' a right fool o' this poor auld wumman. There wis nothin' runnin' doon her chin. An' she wisnae havin' dauds o' white bread sookin' up the broon gravy. She wisnae havin' mince and totties – NOR SOUP!

Josie: Oh, it wis KNORR soup she wis havin'!

Francie: She wis havin' nothin' o' the kind. When I say "nor soup", I mean the granny wisnae havin' soup at all. SHE WIS AT ARBROATH – BUT SHE WIS HAVIN' NOTHIN' – D'YE HEAR ME? THE AULD SCUNNER WIS HUVIN' NOTHIN'!

Josie: Are you tryin' tae tell me that poor auld wumman wis away tae Arbroath wi'out even a sangwich?

Francie: Yes, Josie. Yes, yes, yes. That's the joke, ye see. A chap at the door. "Is yer granny in?" "Naw, she's at Arbroath." "That's alright, Ah'll come in and wait 'til she's feenished." D'ye no' see. He thought she wis in there havin' a plate o' broth – wi' a big ham shank in it. An' she wisnae there at a'.

Josie: Well, that is the stupidest joke Ah've ever . . . AW! AH SEE WHIT YE MEAN! (He goes into paroxysms of laughter . . .)
YOU MEAN THEY HOLD THE SPIRITUALIST MEETIN'S IN SAFEWAYS!!!!!!!

THE END